What they s
Lattes, Laughter and Lipstick

"Just enjoying the ride. I like the way they all approached their homework – very clever how you got all the image stuff in there."

Ronel Fourie – Image Impact group

"We are all part of the spiritual ascension that is occurring now. Use whatever methods necessary to get 'The message across'! Clare's spokeswomen is Joy! Use her!!!"

"Cynthia, you've got it all wrong. You can be loud, but no one has heard you, you can be obvious and no one has seen you. I want you to be real and no one will miss you." ... (Brilliant!!!!) Fabulous chapter Clare ... you do your best work when you're 'being' Joy."

Nicole Jackman – Cerulean Wings

"Clare has taken the angst out of dress fashion and turned it into 'Joy.'

Nancy Vino – retired

Dear Pat,

Thanks for your patience & your support.

Cheers
Clare ☺

Lattes, Laughter and Lipstick

The book that transforms and revitalises women

Clare Maxfield

DISCLAIMER

All the information, techniques, skills and concepts contained within this publication are
of the nature of general comment only and are not in any way recommended as individual
advice. The intent is to offer a variety of information to provide a wider range of choices
now and in the future, recognising that we all have widely diverse circumstances and
viewpoints. Should any reader choose to make use of the information contained herein,
this is their decision, and the contributors (and their companies), authors and publishers
do not assume any responsibilities whatsoever under any condition or circumstances.
It is recommended that the reader obtain their own independent advice.

Published by CMI
55 Norfolk Court, Doncaster, Victoria 3108 Australia
Phone: +61 3 414 339 113 or Fax +61 3 9017 8937

First Edition 2009

Second Edition 2010

Copyright © 2010 by Clare Maxfield.

All rights reserved. No part of this publication may be reproduced, stored in a retrieval
system, or transmitted in any form or by any means, electronic, mechanical, photocopying,
recording or otherwise, without the prior written permission from the publisher.

Produced by Palmer Higgs Pty Ltd
www.palmerhiggsbooks.com.au

National Library of Australia
Cataloguing-in-Publication entry:

  Maxfield, Clare
  Lattes, laughter and lipstick: the book that transforms and
  revitalises women / Clare Maxfield.
  2nd ed. 9780646538044 (pbk.)
  Includes index.
  Self-actualization (Psychology).
  Body image in women.
  Clothing and dress.
  158.1

For Nancy and Ngoc

Clare Maxfield

Contents

About the author

Clare Maxfield lives in the outer suburbs of Melbourne with her husband and two dogs. She is an award winning Image Consultant and international bestselling author with her first book *Getting Gorgeous*. After her beloved Ansett Airlines collapsed in 2002 Clare discovered a talent she never knew she had. She loves to make people feel confident in themself and she loves training. She now runs her own Image consultancy www.claremaxfield.com.au and Image Consultant Training Academy at www.InternationalStyleAcademy.com.au.

Clare writes regularly for the *Good Life – Peninsula Style* and the *Starchoice Magazine* as well as providing articles for many other periodicals. She currently sits on the international board of the Association of Image Consultants International and is one of the first few members holding the designation Certified Image Professional here in Australia. Clare is also a Professional Member of the National Speakers Association of Australia.

Clare has run workshops on image all across Australia, New Zealand, America, Kazakhstan and the Ukraine. Her audiences have ranged from major corporations to teenagers in school. For more information about Clare Maxfield and her programs go to www.ClareMaxfield.com.au

Acknowledgements

This book could not have happened without the support of my good friends and family. I want to send a special thank you to Ronel, for urging me along and knowing when to hang up and when to keep talking on the phone. You never got tired of hearing about the girls, my invisible friends. Nicole who, within hours of a chapter finishing, would give me feedback on what was working for her and what wasn't. Thank you for all of the 'hats' you wore for me. My beautiful friend Niki who knows she is just special to me and, lastly, to my Mum, who has never before been so involved in what I am doing and I think she finally gets it. I knew I had hit the mark when she told me Joy brought her to tears.

Sarah Rogers, thank you for creating those amazing images that start each chapter of the girls' stories. To be able to use your photographs in my book is a wonderful gift. You are a very talented lady. Mel, thank you for being a wonderful model for Sarah to use.

I cannot forget my special team of readers who did the wonderful work of editing this book for me, Di Thomas, Tricia Fidock, Jane Coutts, Martin Shakespeare and Bron Copley. Paul, Debbie and the team at Palmer Higgs who picked me up when I thought this book was going nowhere.

A special thank you goes to my wonderful husband Ngoc who is the most amazing support I could ever imagine.

My final thank you goes to everyone I have ever consulted to in the past. There is a little of everyone's story in these girl's lives.

Chapter 1.

Old friends reunited

Old friends reunited

'Can you hear that?' asked Louise quietly into Rob's warm neck.

'Hear what,' mumbled Rob into his pillow.

'Exactly – the sound of silence.'

With his arm flung casually across the bed Louise watched him with wonderment. For 22 years she had loved this man, shared his bed and given birth to his children. Potentially not in the ideal order as their first child was conceived just as they had finished high school but that did not stain their marriage. It only sped up the inevitable.

This morning Louise woke to the first morning of the rest of her life with her husband Rob and their new life as empty nesters. While her children, Jade and Paul, had both been away for many nights at the same time in the past this morning was different. Yesterday they had put Jade on a flight to Perth to start her studies in Mineral Geosciences at the University of Western Australia and Paul had left only a week earlier for a new position with the accounting firm he worked for in London. This was the first morning that the pair of them had been truly alone in their whole married life. While many said their shotgun marriage straight after school wouldn't last, Louise had never looked back. Louise snuggled into Rob but the elusive sleep-in she was hoping for was overtaken by an overwhelming desire to cook and clean. Theirs had always been a busy social life so the thought of living without their children underfoot only added to the freedom she now felt. Really she had to hold on fast to this feeling otherwise the dread and overwhelming sense of loss and loneliness that the hole her children left would consume her. Her children were her greatest achievement. She loved her family, loved being a wife and adored being a mother. Louise bounded out of bed, planning to get the coffee going before Rob started mumbling his standard morning monotone of, 'Coffee, coffee, coffee.'

These ramblings were as consistent as the tone of his alarm clock. Louise looked around at her bedroom as if for the first time and in some cases hopefully the last time. Their bedding was faded and was that a stain in the corner? Oh yes, that was Jade's attempt to make her breakfast in bed using her doll's kitchen tea set and red cordial. The realisation that this bedding was over 10 years old hit her suddenly.

Where had her focus been for all of these years? When had she last spent time taking care of her life?

'Note to self,' she muttered, 'it is time for a new cover, and while I'm at it I'll get us new pillows, I should update this old manky dressing gown and why not get a new pair of PJs?'

These passion killers had done their job just a bit too effectively over the past few years and it was about time to bring a little glamour back into the bedroom. She almost laughed aloud when she caught her reflection. What was she thinking when she purchased these pyjamas? They were electric blue with lime and purple flowers. Maybe a bit too much coffee that morning. However they were on a sales rack and let's face it, who sees you in bed at night? Rob certainly never noticed what she had on. Rob was simple and reliable. For him it was either a case of roll into bed to read and sleep, or roll into bed to read, then romp and sleep. Either way her clothing or sleep wear had none to little impact on his needs, wants or desires.

With the coffee brewing and her cup of tea in her hand she sat down to read the morning paper. Out of the corner of her eye she looked at the card she had received in the mail only yesterday. It was sitting in the wicker basket at the end of her kitchen bench along with the other odds and ends that needed to be kept but did not have anywhere in particular to be stored. Things like spare pens, rubber bands, grocery receipts and lists. This card was an invitation. Louise and Rob lived a fairly social life so invitations were not a rarity but this one sent shivers of anguish, anticipation and guilt simultaneously down her spine.

Twenty years – how was it possible that so much time had passed yet the memories were as fresh in her mind as if they were yesterday.

The final day of school was a hoot. Cynthia Fullham, Rebecca Mayne and she were never trouble makers but they were a close unit and to the dismay of their teachers a dangerous blend of intelligence and creativity. A dangerous mix. Especially when idle hands are left to do the devil's work old Mrs Matheson the principal would say of the trio. Privately she would look forward to seeing what the girls would come up with next either for a class excursion or an unsanctioned activity. Their final day was no disappointment to her. The planning of this day took months and the whole year level was involved. In many schools around the country the last day or 'muck up day' was a day to be feared. Young men and women on the cusp of adulthood seem to use this day to express their inner child or inner brat to be more precise. Teachers' cars would get covered in shaving foam, homemade flags would be raised on the flag pole, water bombing between the schools is standard. This in itself is another reason why many teachers do not wear their best clothes on the day as the chances of wearing a water bomb followed by a dusting of flour is all too possible.

> ## The Student Social Committee of the Past Pupils Association of Fairview Grammar invites you to attend the 20 year reunion of the Class of 1989.

It was Cynthia's idea that they 'Gnome' the school. The girls discussed it and the whole form got involved. Everyone was to bring three gnomes to school. Unfortunately for the local neighbourhood, many of the gnomes were picked up out of gardens as the girls were passing. The gnomes lived in the bottom of the girls lockers until the last day. Then as one the girls arrived as the sun rose. Every girl had her own tube of glue and they went to work gluing their gnomes around the school. There were gnomes crossing the quadrangle, walking up the stairs, standing outside the staff room, waiting at the library and one at the very front of Mrs Matheson's car park. It ensured that Mrs Matheson did not over park in her spot or the unsuspecting gnome was likely to lose his head. Everyone arrived and roared with laughter at the 336 gnomes scattered around the school. That is until they realised that they were firmly fixed to the ground and moving them wouldn't be as easy as it seemed.

At the conclusion of classes that day Louise went to the beach with Cynthia and Rebecca and a few others but it was those two girls who were definitely and undeniably her best friends. As they sat in the sun, tanning their long legs and drinking UDL vodka and passion fruit which was their drink du jour and ably provided by Cynthia's 18 year old boyfriend, they vowed that no matter what happened the three of them would be friends for life.

It was true they had stayed friends for life. Only last week Louise had posted Cynthia a birthday card. She never forgot a birthday; her well worn birthday book was a great gift from her mum at 16. It may be a bit dog-eared and faded but it still worked. But when had they last seen each other? That would have had to have been Michael's 1st birthday; Rebecca's youngest boy, over 7 seven years ago now. She had planned to invite the girls to both Paul and Jade's 18th birthdays but both children had shrugged off the idea of a big party in favour of a deposit on a car and going to the pub with their mates.

It will be great to see the girls, she knew that. But the guilt over losing contact was gnawing at her the more she thought about the old days. It was the three of them spending summers on the beach at Mentone right in front of the surf lifesaving clubhouse or Mornington at Shire Hall Beach. Then Saturdays during the year at Southland shopping centre (there was no Sunday trading back then), or upstairs smoking on Rebecca's balcony while her parents were downstairs watching telly.

Get over yourself, she thought. Louise was a pacifier. She made sure everyone was happy, fed and clean, possibly the clean part only went as far as her children. Hang on a minute, she suddenly remembered the time Cynthia stayed at her house to go to a blue light disco at the local hall and she came home with grass stains on her shoulders and rather than let her Mum find out she lent her that new top she had got from Just Jeans. Come to think of it she never did get that top back from Cynthia. But then when did anyone ever get anything back from Cynthia?

It was with this thought in mind that she started to look at all of the furnishings in her house and planning the redecoration which should have happened years ago. She loved her secure ordered life. The thing Louise loved about her life was that while Rob and her children brought home all of their problems to her she had created a sanctuary for everyone in this house. It may not look flash but it was their home and even though she and Rob may have the house to themselves now Jade and Paul would always have their rooms to come home to.

Only ten minutes away on the other side of the city but a lifetime away from Louise, Cynthia was dealing with her own early morning problems.

'Phil, I'm going to be late for work. Get out of the shower.'

'Come on sweetheart, five minutes, come and join me. It'll be fun. I'll make up for last night.'

Last night, what a horrific memory that was. Cynthia had been seeing Phil for two months now and she could feel he was nearing his use-by date. What was it with these men? Initially he had been so much fun and so attentive. Let's see, there was that stunning bunch of Asiatic lilies delivered to her at work after the first date, a river cruise for the second date, a night at a small local fringe show for their third date. He had seemed too good to be true. They had enjoyed walks along the Yarra River after late Sunday brunches in the Botanical Gardens. Riding their pushbikes from Port Melbourne to the little café in Brighton right at the end of North Road. Late nights sitting up in his apartment overlooking the shrine on St. Kilda Road discussing politics, entertainment and sport. But then something happened. Cynthia had to go away for a weekend retreat for work and Phil flipped his switch. Thursday night before she left he rode her like he was riding a marathon. Luckily for Cynthia she was away for the weekend to allow her loins to cool, as she grimaced to herself. He then text messaged and emailed her relentlessly all weekend. One, maybe two, even three a day would have been sweet but 50 messages a day was bordering on stalking and the actions of a man losing his mind. As soon as she returned he showered her with flowers again and started saying how much he missed her and how they should move in together. That was two weeks ago and now Cynthia knew it was time to call it quits. The loving level headed man she had met had morphed into a controlling, frightening, obnoxious, territorial madman. Ah, another one bites the dust.

And now of all times. This weekend was her school reunion and she so wanted to tell the girls she had met The One. The keeper, the man of her dreams who would fix all of her problems. Instead she would have to report there was no movement on her marital status and none likely in the near future. Where had all of the good men gone? That's right, they had married her two best friends. With that thought a small furrowing of her brow occurred. Can you still call a woman who you have not spoken to for seven years your best friend? Or even a couple of women you have not spoken to your best friends? In her heart she knew she could. While time may have passed it was only due to the interference of *it* on their lives. You know *it* which happens all of the time. *it* may be good, *it* may be bad, but *it* cannot be denied or ignored when *it* happens. *It* is the unexpected events which colour our lives and cannot be controlled. True friends are always there no matter what. With the comforting thought that she would be seeing her oldest and dearest friends this weekend it was time to focus on the lingering problem in her bathroom.

A smile came to her face as she realised that a farewell bonk is always a fun bonk so why not get into that shower and enjoy it. After all what would it matter if she was a few minutes late for work? Cynthia had had it with her job anyway. She had been with Asquith and Moore, a recruitment firm in Collins Street, Melbourne for the past three years. They had offices all around the world and try as she might she seemed to get nowhere fast. It was not as if she wanted to climb all the way to the top but somehow promotions kept sliding by her. When she joined she had decided this was the time to get serious about her career. She had done really well in all her previous positions but it was now time to make a difference.

Upon reflection Cynthia's 20s had been a blast, as they should be and she had seen relative success early in her life but weren't the 30s for settling down and getting established. Something had gone wrong here. She still didn't own her own place, she was still single and she was still not paid anything like the girls she went through university with. Cynthia tried to get serious about saving for a mortgage but something always got in her way. Last year she almost had her credit cards paid off but the airlines had an amazing deal on travel to London and New York. The shopping was sensational. Then this year, just as she got her cards in order again her car gave her some trouble. She'd had her Honda CRV for five years and then the new twin top cars came out. Having a convertible would be so much nicer in summer than the city dwelling 4WD she currently had. Try as she would to save money just slipped through her fingers.

Every morning is starting to feel like ground hog day to Rebecca. Justin leaves the house at 7am to get into his office and she is left to wake, dress and feed her boys. Jacob at 9 is getting easier to get out of bed but it is Luke who has never been an easy riser. She knows it is partially her fault as she has never insisted that the boys go to bed early. Once they stopped being babies she started to treat them more like adults, in as much as they could chose what clothes they wanted to wear and what co-curricular activities they were interested in. Funny how both boys followed after their father into football. She gave them music and tennis lessons when they were younger but it was football that sparked their interest.

'Jacob, Lucas, get up. DON'T MAKE ME COME AND GET YOU OUT OF BED.' Where had that shrill edge to her voice come from? Rebecca caught her reflection in the mirror as she yelled out to the boys. Hair in a ponytail, loose t-shirt and ¾ length gym pants. Which by the way had not seen the gym for nine years now. Upon closer inspection the pants were starting to wear very thin but were very handy when you had to get up in a hurry to a sick child and didn't want to sit around in your nightgown. Sure her t-shirt had faded but it was still clean and her hair might not be a glossy as it used to be but then she had worn it in a pony tail for the past nine years since the boys were born. Come to think of it when had she last dressed properly? Aside from parties or special events Rebecca's daily dressing style was Easy Care Semi Grunge Mum, certainly not Yummy Mummy Chic. But some of the mothers at school were seriously into that style. Yummy Mummy Chic consisted of clothing that you could move easily in. A step up from gym wear but co-ordinated enough so that if they met up in the street they could easily stop for coffee. Their bodies were trim from working out at the gym and their make-up applied just so that the harried expression brought on by motherhood was expertly veiled by a glow of mineral make-up and lip gloss. Rebecca liked these women, it was not as if they weren't nice people, but she had always been so busy with her boys. She couldn't understand where they found the time or the energy to focus on themselves. Those were the days. Rebecca thought back to her days before the boys. She had the time to go to the gym, apply face masks and put hair treatments in her hair. Those were the days when Justin would hold her close as he breathed in her hair and hold it for a second as her marvelled at his good fortune to have Rebecca Mayne fall in love with him. Before the boys her life had been completely different. Rebecca was a stunning woman, in fact she still was. Only now she didn't fuss as much with her appearance and if the truth was told she didn't have to as she was still a very attractive woman. She could still frock up well given the right occasion and even Justin seemed to have settled into fatherhood just as she had motherhood with a slight thickening of his waist as well.

'Jacob, Lucas I mean it. Come on it's time for school. You are going to miss your bus if you don't hurry. I suppose I can take you if you want to lie in bed a bit longer.'

It was instantaneous the sound of fear and scrambling. The boys had become very self-sufficient in the past six months and the thought of Mum dropping them off to school was frightening to them. It wasn't that they were doing or planning anything wrong but they had had a taste of independence and they liked it. Growing up was fun for them and while they loved and adored their mother, frankly, she was no longer necessary for them to hold onto out in public. At home it was a different matter but their mates didn't need to know that. Rebecca was relishing watching her boys grow and develop but a corner of her heart was sad with the knowledge that her little boys wouldn't crawl into her lap for cuddles any more or rely on her being there for them.

What to do, what to do, what to do with her day? The thought of her school reunion gave her something to focus on. This will be great she thought, now what am I going to wear? Rebecca knew that once the boys had left the house, after she had cleared away the breakfast dishes, made the beds and put a load of washing on she had a couple of options left to do with her time. She could vacuum again or she could go out shopping for a new outfit to wear to the reunion. This would require something very special. She wanted to look fabulous, not frumpy. Her figure had altered substantially since school and dressing it hadn't exactly caused her a challenge but she never felt the same spark of invincibility that she had when she was younger. Being a mother was wonderful but where had Rebecca gone. She felt invisible these days. She knew if she told Justin he would laugh at her as he still saw the gorgeous girl he married every night when he came home from the office and the boys would run into the house and throw themselves at their mother and talk over each other excitedly as they told her how great their day had been. With a shake of her head and a smile to herself she shook off the feeling as she knew her life was blessed.

Chapter 2.

He left me

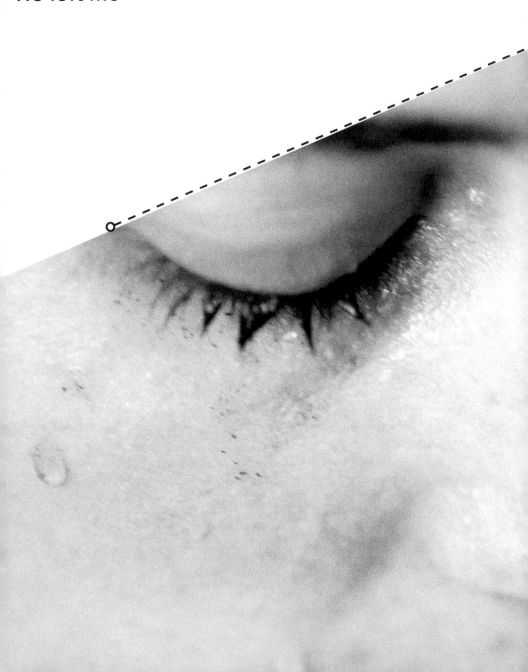

He left me

The reunion was more fun than any of the girls could ever have planned. It was as if time had stood still for them. They reconnected as they hadn't in years and each woman felt as if that little piece of her that had been gone for so long was rediscovered in the connection with her old friends from school. After the reunion they decided that they would not leave it so long to catch up so they found a coffee shop that was central to all of them and started catching up every other Thursday. At first it was tough for Cynthia to get away from work but she discovered she could flex her hours and have a half day off on Thursdays. She had the hours to make up but it was only an extra 30 minutes on her other days. It really was a win-win situation for everyone. After the comments about the bosses sister's jacket she knew she was going nowhere fast in that office and was biding her time until she found a better job. How was she to know that the woman she was openly putting down at the water cooler was related to the boss. Anyway, she still thought the jacket she had on was repulsive and so last decade.

After nine glorious months of catching up over coffees and the odd glass of wine the girls were settling into a very comfortable routine. They had been opening up to each other in ways only true girlfriends would open up. So it was an ordinary Thursday in an ordinary week that found them all together in what was now a most ordinary of settings. Only there was nothing ordinary about today.

'He left me.'

The words lay on the table like a dirty dishcloth. They all knew they were there but no one wanted to touch them.

Slowly Louise lifted her head, her eyes filled with pain and abandonment.

'I mean it. He lied to me. You know all of that travel Rob has been doing? Well most of it has been to stay with his mistress, his masseuse in Moonee Ponds. The two of them have been at it for the past two years. No wonder his back was so stuffed!' The words ripped out of her filled with acid.

Cynthia inclined her head, raised her expertly shaped eyebrow and focused in on Louise. 'Louise, I don't get it. The two of you? I mean, we thought that of all couples you and Rob were the most solid. Sorry Rebecca, I know you and Justin are good but Louise and Rob; well they were Louise and Rob, together from school, forever and ever and all that stuff.' The words drifted away as Cynthia felt before she saw the sharp look of reproach Rebecca snapped at her. For once she stopped talking.

With the gentleness that comes from a natural inclination to care for others Rebecca took Louise's hand and asked what they could do.

'Bobbitt him,' Cynthia responded. 'You know slice his pickle, feed his nuts to the squirrels, emancipate him!'

'I think you mean emasculate him,' Louise said quietly and followed that with a small chuckle. 'Cynthia, there are no squirrels in Australia but we could feed his nuts to the sharks. Oh hell, why stop at his nuts. Throw the whole lot in.'

'So is there any hope of his going back? Would you take him back if he asked,' Rebecca asked with a question in her voice.

'Let me think about that for a minute? No, never and absolutely not!' came Louise's quick and firm response. 'We have hardly been more than roommates if I think about it for the past six or seven years. When the kids were small every weekend we would go and do something together. Nights we were too tired to think but as they got older I became the chief cook, cleaner, taxi and diary clerk. If I wasn't driving one to netball, I was taking the other to football or cricket, arranging Rob's dry cleaning and then the weekends revolved around their sports, and parties. Rob and I stopped existing as a couple as the kids took over my life and work took over his.'

'Lou you sound like any normal mother. My goodness your life sounds exactly as I imagine mine and Justin's will end up like. Are you saying this is my future too?'

'Bec, what do you see when you look at Justin? Is he the man you adore or just the sperm donor for your children? Do you still have that early spark; that tingle when you hear his voice or say his name?'

'Well when you put it that way. Although sometimes I'm so tired from the boys I hardly feel alive. Lucky for me breathing is automatic or I reckon I'd stop some nights. But definitely Justin is still the hunk I married and sometimes I cannot believe how much more I love him now that we have the boys.'

'Good on you Bec. Rob and I never had that. Rob and I loved each other don't get me wrong but we married for the wrong reasons. We were young, I was pregnant, and we were having fun. So we thought why not? I was a good Mum; I am a good Mum, that's all I know how to do. I was never really his wife. We were parents, we played our roles well and our roles are just over as our marriage is.'

'So what now Lou? What are you planning? Live a life of leisure, prowl nightclubs and pick up young boys, or hang out in bars being the gay divorcée…'.

It was with utterance of the D word that Cynthia realised that she had, true to form, gone too far. Louise lost focus in her eyes and stared ahead of herself into a dim future.

'Lou, I'm sorry, I didn't mean that. You are way too classy for that and I never, well, I didn't mean anything. But well, are you guys going to get a divorce? Have you thought about it?'

As the words spewed from Louise's lips the girls knew exactly how she felt. 'You bet I am. That arsehole has strung me along for long enough. It's my turn now!'

'You go girl,' said Cynthia relieved that she hadn't totally destroyed the mood of the moment. For the rest of the afternoon the girls drank their lattes and discussed Louise's new life without Rob. They discussed all that she had to look forward to. It was a pleasant afternoon and they all looked forward to catching up again in two weeks.

'He left me.'

Astonishment struck Louise and Cynthia simultaneously as Rebecca delivered these three words.

Louise's left hand flew to her mouth as her right hand sought out that of her friends arm. Her eyes grew wide and her face paled. Cynthia sat in silence. After the close call of their previous catch-up where she nearly delivered some of her finest faux pas's to Louise she decided this was not the time to start talking.

Rebecca looked from face to face and realised what she had said. Hurriedly she tried to clarify her comment. 'No not Justin, my baby. Luke. I thought you would remember I had said today Luke would have to come with me as he had a free day from school only he left me to catch up with his friends to go to the movies. They are growing up so fast these days.'

The relief was palpable between Louise and Cynthia. Louise and Rob splitting up was bad enough but if Rebecca and Justin separated then there was no future for mankind.

'Well then I guess I had better be the one to say it next,' said Cynthia.

'Say what?' chimed Louise and Rebecca

'He left me,' announced Cynthia with a sigh.

'Who left you?' Louise's forehead creased as she tried to place what Cynthia was saying.

'Phil.'

'Which one was Phil?' countered Rebecca.

'The architect.'

'I thought you dumped him just before the reunion?' asked Rebecca

Louise was not so delicate, 'Cynthia, darling, you know we love you but you're a bum magnet.'

'Phil wasn't a bum. He shopped on Chapel Street.'

'So he was a well educated, well dressed, emotional loser then.' Louise smirked as Rebecca nodded her head in agreement at her comments. Even Cynthia had to join in on the laughter. Her love life was a dismal failure and the girls all agreed that it's not as if she was loose, because she genuinely fell in love with every one of her boyfriends. They just didn't fall in love with her.

'Cynthia whatever happened to Fabio?' At the mention of his name the girls fell into fits of laughter. At her 30th birthday Cynthia was dating Tim, a real estate agent who spent more time looking at his own reflection than at her or anyone else for that matter. Even her neighbours commented on the time he took to climb the stairs to her apartment. He spent most of the time checking his appearance before knocking on her door. Poor guy, this was one of the few occasions when she took the initiative and did the dumping. After a string of messages from his pager to hers about how he was busy in the office it was all too clear that he was clearing the decks for her replacement. Cynthia sent him a response not to call, page or bother her any more. Then the girls opened another bottle of chardonnay and giggled the evening away. He was no great loss.

'Don't worry girls, I am off men! I am going to focus on my work and enjoy being single again.' Cynthia declared confidently.

This last comment brought fresh smiles to her friends faces as both girls knew Cynthia did not do single well.

'Stop it. I mean it! My plan is to get that promotion I have let slip through my fingers, lose five kilos and then find my Mr Wonderful.' This only led to more laughter. 'So you think I can't do it huh.'

'Cyn, you have been wanting a better job, a better man and to lose those five kilos since we left school. Firstly I want to know where you want to lose those five kilos from, but you have been singing this same tune for years from the same microphone.' Louise used no malice as she was purely stating that which they all knew and had commented on many times in the past.

Switching the conversation away from herself Cynthia spoke to Louise. 'So how's it going in your world Lou?'

'Not good I am afraid.' Louise dryly responded.

'Rob being a schmuck?' Cynthia probed.

'You could say that. We're broke.'

'Broke,' the girls chimed in unison.

'Yep, stone, motherless broke to be exact.'

'Hang on a minute. Didn't you just nab a huge contract with one of the major retailers?' Rebecca couldn't help herself, this was too much.

'Yes but that huge contract cost us greatly to fit-out the warehouse to run the quantities they were after and now with the downturn all we are left with is the first and second mortgage on our house, full warehouses and empty pockets.'

'But surely you can sell that stuff.'

'Yeah Cyn, we can but it is going to take time and we can't eat the homewares he imported. Anyway Miss Masseuse has told him he should stop worrying about the financial chaos, that it is only a manifestation of the troubles that he and I are sharing and that the sooner he and I are through the better. His finances will improve and he will be free to create whatever reality he really wants to create for himself.'

'Have you got any savings?' quietly questioned Cynthia finally, as the enormity of not just Louise losing Rob but her entire life savings was starting to dawn on the girls. Especially since she had never had any savings but always assumed that those two, the steady ones, would have everything forever.

'Some, but just enough to pay the second mortgage. Rob's going to take care of the first mortgage and give me the house but there is nothing left to live on. I'm just going to have to get a job. So girls tell me. What the hell does a 39 year old woman, whose qualifications are cooking, cleaning and ferrying around teenagers do? I have no skills, no clothes, nothing. I'm irrelevant.'

'Louise, stop it you are amazing,' said Rebecca.

'Thanks Becs, but at what?'

'Well as a person, you are a doer, you don't let things get to you.'

'Bec, I've known I had no money for six months. I can't say I've exactly been doing anything up 'til now.'

Cynthia had one of her moments of clarity, 'You know what?'

'No, what?' came their response in unison.

'We need to do something to make our lives better. I don't know, what say we go and see a psychic and depending on what they say make our plans. Either way we have started something.'

'Yeah, yeah, yeah, yeah, yeah ... you girls are all talk and no action.'

'I beg your pardon!' Louise had not raised two children without learning a thing or two about being spoken back to and this sounded as if she was being spoken back to.

They had been coming to the Café Club for almost a year now and this was the first time that Joy the owner had piped up into their conversation. Had she been listening this whole time?

All heads swivelled as if in one motion and three sets of eyes bored into the quiet unassuming eyes of the woman behind the counter. Her hair was softly pulled back into a low bun, her clothing was simple and she had the expression of a saint. So what right did she have to comment on their conversation? This was not a declaration of war yet but she had better explain herself and explain herself fast. You don't enter into the inner sanctum of a ring of girlfriends without good reason.

'I said, you girls are all talk and no action. You are like a Chinese meal. You walk out of here filled with promise and commitment and half an hour later have forgotten everything you have promised each other and gone back to your comfortable ways without making any change or any effort.'

'Joy,' said Cynthia, 'you know we love coming here but part of the reason we come here is because no one knows us, we can say what we like and no one will judge us no matter what. We don't have to be anyone to anyone.'

'Yep and that is your problem. I have been listening to you girls ever since you started coming here and at first it was just because you were sitting there that I kept the music low so you could hear each other speak. But the down side is that often I can also hear you. My hair may be grey and my body heading south on me but my ears still work fine.'

Joy learned towards the group, putting down her notepad and pencil. She knew it was time to open up to them. To see if these girls had the guts to make the changes she knew they could make if only they had someone to show them. Just as she had had someone show her not so long ago. That is if you count sixty years as not so long ago.

Joy Alice Bell, was born in a different era. Life wasn't necessarily easier or harder but it was certainly simpler and she was one of the very lucky ones. She had finished school, had a successful modelling career, married a wonderful man who adored her, travelled the world with him and was settling into her happily ever after when at 65 he died suddenly of a heart attack. Money was never going to be an issue but she was still young. She was only 62 when he died and a young 62 at that. She had a lot of living to go and was not going to spend it idly. It was then she opened the Café Club. The Café Club was her opportunity to keep active. Whilst she loved her married life and the travel, she had always been a people person and this gave her the opportunity to mix with different people every day. During the day she served coffee, cake and foccacias. Then at night she served the after work crowd. It was mainly Chablis and Cab Savs but occasionally there would be someone wanting to celebrate something and she would make them one of her famous burnt orange margaritas.

She was asked daily how she made the burnt orange flavour and her response was, 'that's my little secret,' but surely if they thought about it they could figure it out. Grab the orange peel and sear it over an open flame. Squeeze orange juice into the sugar crystals and reduce in a hot pan, and then add white rum. Most nights she closed the bar at about 10pm as it was not an all night venue. Just a comfortable place to stop on the way home. She had designed the interior to reflect the varying moods of her clientele. There were bar stools for the newcomers who weren't too sure of the lay of the land. She had standard tables against a banquette that ran along the far wall and chairs set up in groups of four. And a select few sets of tables had tub chairs in a deep chocolate brown for those who wanted to feel like they were at home. These girls had taken to sitting in the setting in the furtherest corner from the door but right next to the far end of the bar where Joy just happened to do her paperwork. Up 'til now they thought they were invisible and for the most part they were. But what they didn't know is that whilst they could not see or hear Joy writing away in her accounts book she could hear everything they said. For the majority of the time she hadn't listened at all, but as their happy reunion had started dissolving into a mess of lost love, broken dreams and disillusionment with life she couldn't help herself any longer. Her mothering instinct kicked in and she wanted to help these girls. She was only where she was in life because she had someone with her who never put her in the shadow of his life. Her Tom gave her the confidence to speak up and to be confident in who she was. True he said she collected sad souls and set them free again but, well, what was another three souls saved. She wasn't getting involved where she had no knowledge, she could see and hear these girls' pain and if she could help well help she would.

'Now I hear you when you say you like coming here because no one knows you and you can be yourselves but I have to ask you. Does anybody really know you? In fact do you know yourself and when did you all become invisible?'

Cynthia's eyes lifted to the ceiling not in attitude of here we go again but Rebecca felt a subtle acceptance of what Joy was saying. She knew what it felt like to be invisible in fact ever since she had given birth to her first child had she become invisible. All she ever talked about was her kids, what they did what they achieved, what they needed. Her and Justin had not had a conversation about anything except the kids for almost nine years now. Unless of course they were discussing his job, because all her day entailed was being a Mum. She organised the house, the tradesmen, the kids' tennis, the kids' music lessons, and the kids' school holiday. What had happened to her life? She was thirty and fabulous once.

Only nine years ago Rebecca was a flight attendant. She had joined the airlines straight after school and travelled the friendly skies till the day she resigned to start her family. That was before terrorism and price wars. Those were the days when the flight attendants were able to give service and not the type of service some celebrities look for in locked toilets. She had travelled not just all around Australia but most of the world. Jetting off with her friends on her holidays to see Asia, Europe, Africa, Egypt, America – you name it she went there. It was nothing to fly to Perth or Sydney for lunch if her friends were on a trip and lay-over's in Darwin during the winter ensured she always had a tan. She spent her 30th birthday in Bali with 15 of her nearest and dearest and some extras too. She had her own flat, her own car, her own money and a man who loved her dearly. What could be better than that? Yep, a family. Rebecca had no qualms about giving up the pill to start a family. She had been married four years by then. A baby would make her life complete. To be honest the children had been the best decision Rebecca had ever made, but the impact on her life and her body was completely unexpected. She was the first of her flying friends to have a baby so it was all new to them all. Initially everyone came by to have a chat and a catch up and look at her beautiful baby but as time wore on the visits became less and less and the pull on her life by the children became more and more especially when the second baby came only two years later. Again he was planned but no one prepared her for the shouting, the screaming, the nappies, the sleepless nights. The overall intensity of the situation. She knew once they started school it would change and it did but again she was locked into their power as it was expected at the school as that she would help out in the canteen. Inevitably she ended up on the committee and eventually running the canteen. It was no wonder as a flight attendant she had been a cabin manager so running a meal service whether it was 16,000 metres in the air or in a primary school couldn't be too different. What she had never expected was to become so invisible to the world. She was the boys' mother or her husband's wife but it had been years since she had been Rebecca. The glamazon of the air. True she did have an amazing figure back then but two boys had been the finish of that, well, that's what she told herself. Where had that cottage cheese on her thighs come from and how was it that her once pert bum had morphed into two full moons of glowing contentment? Her flat stomach now moved independently of her body when she ran and don't let her get started on her upper arms. The boys thought it was a great game last summer to watch the skin swing back and forward when she was trying to read her book on holidays. Brats and beasts they were and if she hadn't been there when they emerged from her womb she may have questioned if they were really related to her or not. Yes she knew what it felt like to be invisible.

'I say all of this with love so hear me out if you will. Louise, my dear, I cannot believe you have been sitting here for months knowing that not only your marriage but your finances were going down the toilet. Rob, well he was a case unto himself and it sounds as if you should have left him before he left you but either way he is no great loss. However you could have put something in place to protect your income and your savings. Nothing to be done with that now but your stoic approach to saving everyone from your woes has potentially cost you. Now that it is out in the open you can turn your life around. When you stop being an enabler you will be amazed at how much others can do for them and how much time and energy you have for yourself.'

Louise nodded slowly at Joy's words and the other girls sat back in thought. Joy was by no means finished though.

'Rebecca, it is time to stop hiding behind your boys. From what I hear they are happy, they are well cared for and they are growing up. You have got yourself lost in their world. When was the last time you did something for yourself? You complain about your shape and looking dreadful in everything. Well, wake up, you are still gorgeous. So you think you are just carrying a bit of weight! well aren't we all. Didn't you used to work out religiously on the treadmill? Get yourself working again for the mental stimulation if nothing else. I know you don't want to go back to the airlines but what else can you do? It was not just about serving tea and coffees. Your skills are greater than you give yourself credit for. Start thinking outside the square and see what you can come up with. It is time to join the world again. And you Miss Cynthia don't think you get off too easily.'

Cynthia sheepishly looked up at Joy as if her mother was addressing her. Come to think of it Joy could be her mother. The thought was comforting and disconcerting all at once. When had her mother ever given her any advice in her life?

'You are smarter than you give yourself credit for. I wonder if you really want this promotion the way you come and go from work as you see fit. I've heard the way you talk about other staff members which leads me to believing you no doubt say the same things at work which is most likely getting back to your boss. You spend way too much time focusing on how you look when I know you know that you look good and last, but not least, you eat men for breakfast and I don't mean that in the nice way. If they are nice you devour them and if they are wrong you desire them. Wake up, the right man is out there but let him find you.'

'Yes, each of you is invisible. Louise you have never looked at yourself, Rebecca you have hidden behind all of the men in your family large and small and Cynthia, you at times are as loud as a two year old throwing a tantrum so everyone has simply tuned you out of their lives. If you girls are prepared to accept my challenge to make a change in your lives we can have some fun and you can rediscover who you are and make those changes I keep hearing you discuss.'

The girls looked at each other warily at first. This was not what they had planned but then there were so many changes going on in each of their lives that their lives were also not exactly as they had planned them. They had very little to lose. If it didn't work out the worst that would happen would be that they would have to find a new coffee shop. And who knows, Loveable Joy may know a thing or two about life.

Louise spoke for the girls.

'Okay Joy, you reckon you can help us out. We are in your hands. What do you want us to do?'

Joy breathed in deeply and slowly. Her eyes scanned each of the faces looking up at her. The moment had come. It was time to make the lives of these women a reflection of their true potential. She was pleased she had hoped this moment would come. 'All right ladies, let's do it this way. I know you girls enjoy coming here and I love having you. Let's say you keep coming here every fortnight as you do only I'll have some exercises for you to do each time. It'll take about three months but I promise you that you will notice real change in your lives.'

The girls weighed up individually what was happening in their lives and figured that there was nothing to lose. They exchanged looks between themselves, nodded imperceptibly to anyone but themselves and announced in unison, 'Okay, we'll do it.'

'Alright, here is your task for next time. Cynthia, you had the right idea in that you lot need to make a plan to improve your lives but I think you can all do better than the psychic on this occasion. When you set your goals you set your purpose. You know the path that you should be on and you have a vision for that path you should be on. How can you know if you have achieved your dreams and desires if you don't know what they are? Simply going on a journey is nice but pointless if you have no plan. I can hear those who like to live on the edge saying that goals are pointless, allow life to toss at you what it will. That is fine but who knows what will get tossed your way. Often this is not what you want, need or desire. Many times though we get caught up in the "woe is me" mentality. I'm a failure, nothing goes right. Think I'll just sit in the corner and mope. Better still I'll go and tell all of my friends so that they too can agree what a loser I am. Then I can feel good that everyone agrees with me and then feel even lousier that I am identified as a complete loser. This is ideal for those looking for a pity party. As humans we crave the acceptance of those around us so often by rising to the top we can slide out of the comfort of our ordinary existence and feel we will lose the connection with our peers. Rubbish. Get over yourself and get on with your own life. Believe me they won't be dragging you with them as they fulfil all of their goals in life. Louise, I want you to think about the sort of work you like doing. List for me what you can and can't do as well as what you will and won't do. Try and give me a picture of your ideal life if you can while you are at it. Dream big as you are in a position to make it any way you want right now. Rebecca, we need to get you visible again in your mind so if you could focus on how you spend your time as well as your eating patterns for me that would be great. And Cynthia, you said you wanted a promotion, a man and to lose the five kilos. Well you can forget the diet honey, you'll vanish into thin air if you lose any weight. Make a list of your value to your company, your desired position and what those people are doing. For now I need you to stick with your plan to stop chasing men as they are diluting your focus. Alright, be off with you all now. You have work to do and don't imagine that this is going to be easy.'

Chapter 3.

Who are you?

Who are you?

Thursday dawned chilly with a light fog in the air. Joy looked forward to seeing her girls as she now thought of the trio arriving for their coffee and the reawakening that was ahead of them. It had been so long since she had had a side project of her own that she was also excited. The café was great but working with people to find their true potential had always been a gift for her. Didn't her own William tell her that she should have been a teacher? He had loved the way his Joybell could make anyone see themselves in a better light. He always said it was because the light shone from within her and lit up the world around her. She missed him dearly but there was nothing to be done about that.

At exactly 2pm the trio arrived together. You could have heard the three of them coming down the street before they even opened the door from the noise they were making.

'Exactly, that is exactly right. I added up all of the food that I was eating and I am surprised I am not the size of a house,' said Rebecca as she slid into her favourite chair, which faced into the room with her back to the window. Rebecca had no interest in what was happening in the world outside. So by sitting with her back to the street she was able to focus on her friends and not be distracted. Lord knows the boys were a total distraction at home and anywhere else she dared to take them. It was not just recently, they had been a handful since birth. She had in her handbag a folder, which she had grabbed from Justin's desk, and loads of lined paper to take her notes on. She felt as if she was returning to the world and she was excited.

'Bec's you have got to be exaggerating?' questioned Louise who could never think ill of anyone.

'Alright let me show you just what I ate in one day.'
Morning – 2 coffees with milk and one sugar,
One muffin with Vegemite and butter,
Orange juice,
Half a piece of toast with strawberry jam. – Luke didn't finish his toast.
Mid morning – latte with one sugar,
Savoury muffin with butter
Lunch – apple juice,

Salad sandwich,
Slice of tea cake I made the night before
Mid afternoon – fruit plate,
Latte with one sugar
Dinner – two of Jake's fish fingers,
Cheese and biscuits before dinner,
3 crumbed lamb cutlets,
Mashed potatoes with lashings of butter,
Green salad,
Apple pie with cream and ice-cream,
Coffee with milk and sugar,
Piece of chocolate,
Two glasses of red wine

'Before I look too closely that is five teaspoons of sugar just in my coffees alone. Then there are the snacks. What hope do I have if I have my nose in the feedbag all day? Joy, I'm amazed. That simple exercise made me see what I was doing all day every day. It also helped me to see how much time I spent fluffing around after the boys. Do you know I vacuum the boys' rooms every day? No wonder I have no time for anything else.'

'So Rebecca what are you going to do differently now that you have this information?'

'For a start I am going to cut out the sugar in my coffee and limit myself to one sweet snack during the day. That alone should help me to lose weight. But as well as the change in my eating pattern I am going to walk three times a week once the boys have left home. With the amount of time I was spending in their rooms cleaning and folding and doing their ironing I can spend my time only ironing twice a week and vacuuming twice a week. Sorry they are boys and they are grubs so I don't think I could make it only once a week, but still that has immediately given me more time for me.'

'Well done. Now Louise, how did you go with your homework this week?' Joy moved her focus to Louise. Louise sat as she always did in the chair against the wall looking into the room. Louise needed to know that everyone was okay. That if anyone needed help she could jump up from her seat and help in an instant. It was a habit that came from always making sure if her family came by that she saw them.

'I don't know. I did everything you said but I can't seem to come up with any solutions like Bec did.'

'Let me be the judge of that,' said Joy comfortably as Louise looked at her as a nervous school girl may the teacher when she is waiting for a judgment on her first essay.

'Okay, but it sounds silly to me. You asked me to list what I did and didn't like to do and what I would and wouldn't like to do and you asked me to describe my dream life. That was easy.'

Joy looked up over her glasses at Louise. 'Easy. You had trouble outlining what you like and don't like but had no problems dreaming up a life for yourself? I suppose that shouldn't surprise me at all. You are so used to making everyone else's life easy that you have forgotten what is important to you in reality but are happy to drift off into a little fantasy if you feel it is removed from fact.'

Louise fidgeted in her seat. This really was like sitting in the class-room at school. There were so many nerves this conversation was hitting that parts of her felt quite raw. But she was going to make this change. Unaccustomed as she was to focusing on herself she gave the back of her neck a nervous scratch and held up her piece of paper to read to the girls her list.

'What I like to do: I like gardening, keeping my house clean, emailing my kids, reading murder mystery stories and walking along the beach alone with my dogs. What I don't like to do: knitting, wearing high heels, dinner parties, I prefer a BBQ and I hate inane small talk with people I don't like. You girls are the exception but then I like you lot.' Laughter filled the small space then the reality of Louise's world was slowly reaching them. She wasn't the loud gregarious girl she had been in school any more. A more subdued Louise had replaced her. A Louise more intent on quiet peaceful activities than parties and drinking. But then had she ever been. Considering she had fallen pregnant straight after school they took her staying at home to be because of the children not because of her own desires.

'Okay Louise, keep going, tell us now what you can and can't do and lastly what your ideal life looks like.' Joy had a way of keeping everything and everyone on track. But they were yet to fully realise this.

'Alright, as to what I can or will do. I'd love to work outdoors, I don't mind weekends but I don't like evenings. I don't mind nine to five but I don't want to go into the city and work in a huge building. I like to dress smart but I don't want to have to wear stockings, I don't even own any, or high heels every day for that matter. If it is important I will put them on. Now to my dream life. Here goes ...'. With this Louise gave a small flourish and bowed to her audience of three.

Joy acknowledged silently for all of her introspection there was a little actress hiding inside of Louise. If only she could somehow release this side of her. But time will tell if there is true potential here she thought.

'My perfect life, by Louise Smart. I am happy. Every day I get out into my garden which is filled with flowering natives and succulents. Yes we are in a drought and I am being water wise with my imaginary garden. I eat my breakfast sitting in the small table in the corner of my kitchen overlooking my garden with floor to ceiling windows. There is an easel in the corner of my living room and I am sketching wildflowers in pencil and there is a telescope on my balcony from where I can see the boats on the bay. God knows how I will ever afford an apartment on the Esplanade but Joy did say to dream so I am dreaming girls!'

'My lounge room has a feature wall in café latte and the television hides behind a cabinet and only comes out for programs of interest otherwise it is off and hidden. Rob had it on all the time whether he was watching it or not. I hate the television. In the evenings I walk my dogs and in winter when it is too dark or cold to walk the dogs at night I sit in front of my open fire and sketch or read. I am happy and I do not answer to anyone else. That is my life. The End.'

The girls were all silent. They knew that the life Louise described was fantasy as the description fitted neither her existing house nor her life, yet sounded perfectly natural for her. They had forgotten that she was the artist in school. Louise was always scribbling in the edges of her books something she had seen or something that took her interest. There was that summer she made them all small framed pictures for Christmas. Small caricatures of them in front of a stylised house. Rebecca tried in vain to remember where she had hers, Cynthia, however knew exactly. Her picture was hanging on her kitchen wall. It was packed safely every time she moved. It reminded her of a time when life was easy and there was everything to live for.

Louise interrupted the girls' trip down memory lane to their paintings with her continued speech.

'So I am no closer to what I should do with myself but at least I know where I want to be doing it.' And with that Louise put down her paper and sat back in her seat.

Joy could see an ideal future for Louise from her notes but it was for Louise to discover. Not her to tell. Instead she opted for a cryptic response.

'Louise, your future will bloom before you. You don't even realise yet but you have planted the seed and you will find what is ideal for you. Just nurture yourself. That is more important now. Come to understand yourself and know that if you want that house on the bay you will get it or if you don't get the house by the bay you may get a better option with all of the warmth and love that you described in that house only somewhere completely unexpected.'

'Great Joy, Rebecca, can see in an instant where she needs to change and you are telling me to sit in my garden. That is not going to feed me.'

'We'll see,' finished Joy for her. 'Sometimes goal setting is about finding instant clarity, other times it is about setting intent and you do not know what will come of your thoughts. If you have placed your desires out there clearly enough the results will formulate in the way that will work best for you and your dreams, which is why I asked you to dream big. You can go home tonight and keep adding to your list. Dreams and goals can grow. They are not static.'

All that was left now was for Cynthia to go over what she had been doing for the past fortnight. Cynthia had her leather bound folder in front of her. Her compendium that held her notes and her life. With a flick of her wrist she opened the clasp to reveal the contents to her table. Inside the compendium were typed sheets with dominant headings and little else.

'My task was to document my value to the company in order to get a promotion. Well this was something I had never thought of before and can I tell you it surprised me. Before you are three sheets of paper. One is entitled Janice Jones, she beat me to the punch with the past promotion. She is my inspiration. The next is my value on which you will see there is a lot of blank space and finally what I have to do to appear valuable. This last one was not too difficult. I had listened to a speaker on first impressions and she mentioned that we impact on people from five areas of influence so I decided to look at every one of the five areas and break them down to ensure that I was meeting exactly the requirements of my intended job. It may seem overkill but I need to know what I should be doing to ensure that I do it right.'

'I'm really interested in what you have there. Can we see it Cyn?' piped up Louise.

'I thought you might so I brought each of you a copy, and I got one for you too Joy. You never know when this info might be useful.' Out of her case Cynthia pulled the following page for each woman.

Visual

Appearance	*Body Language*
Physical appearance	Mannerisms
Clothes	Stance
Grooming	Gestures
	Facial expressions
	Space
	Posture
	Motion

Non visual

Reputation	*Communication*	*Presence*
Visibility	Articulation	Natural self
Track record	Tonality	Rapport
Experience	Vocal variety	Charisma
Qualifications	Language	Confidence
Ethics	Writing style	Self assurance
Values	Listening style	Self esteem
Etiquette	Thinking style	Warmth
	Humour	

'This is a great list but how do you intend to use it? I can see how parts of it will help you but really doesn't most of it say the same thing?' asked Rebecca. 'For instance the final column, you have charisma, rapport, confidence, self-assurance, self esteem. How are they that different and what are you going to do about each one because, girlfriend, you don't have to worry about confidence that's for sure.' With that Rebecca gave her best home girl head rattle and wiggled her finger at Cynthia. Rebecca could be such a dag at times. The girls all laughed. Joy looked on, prompting Cynthia to keep talking.

'I had a long hard look at myself after we last caught up. And saw where I was going. Nowhere fast. I haven't changed since high school. Still the same old Cynthia Fulham or Cynful, the sinful good time girl. I started believing my own marketing. I have been able to pull the guys any time I wanted, get any job I wanted as long as it wasn't too serious and live my life as I saw fit. The reality is starting to come home that I never grew up. My God if I was one of the boys from school I'd be middle aged, with a pony tail and driving around in my wagon with a surf board still roped in place.' The fact that Cynthia was sitting there with a pony tail in her hair did not escape notice from any of the others but they allowed her to move on as it sounded as if she was making some headway in her life.

'I can't make small changes here, I need to do a full 180 on my life. I need to inspect it from every angle, dissect what is working really well and fix what is not. I know I was treating my life and especially my job with little to no respect. I'm lucky I even have a job and if I don't do something fast I won't have one soon so it is time to do something. So yes those words may sound similar but if we look closely at that particular column you asked I'll tell you how I see it. We'll start by focusing on Natural self – that's what am I like when I am not thinking. Rapport – how easily do I relate to those around me? Charisma – what influence do I have on those around me? Confidence – well that speaks for itself but it made me think; am I as confident as I pretend to be or am I fooling no one but myself. That was a biggie for me. I'm still not too sure about that one so we'll come back to it later. Self assurance – this I related very closely to confidence only I rated myself higher here as I am pretty sure of myself and my ability to bluff even the biggest bluffer. Self esteem – ah, here I think again I don't give myself the credit I am due so I fluff around to hide this and I am sure I am hiding nothing from the bosses. And lastly there was Warmth. I hope you think that I am?'

Everyone was amazed at the depth of Cynthia's awareness and her motivation to make changes in both her life and herself. This was something that no one had even considered as part of the process. It was like unpeeling an onion and discovering another layer beneath. That whilst it was easy to remove it could bring tears to your eyes as you did so. Especially if you sliced it with a blunt knife. It appeared Cynthia was peeling her layers slowly and fully digesting what was there at each level.

'Cynthia, I can't believe I am hearing this from you. Does this mean we have said goodbye to the old Cynthia? No more party girl, the wanton woman always wantin' more. As you have said on more than one occasion.'

'Don't worry Lou. Only one step at a time. I still went out last night, had a few drinks; only this time I didn't bring anyone home with me. Though there was this nice looking guy, but I didn't go near him. I listened to Joy and thought I would take it easy. I should have taken it as easy on the red wines though. Bit of a headache this morning. I just did what I had to do today, lucky it's my half day.'

'You three have made great progress in such a short time. Can you see how by focusing on what you want you are starting to see what you don't need any more?' Joy was surprised at the ease with which she had their attention again. She was curious as to how easy these three women were going to make this exercise for her. She did have a knack though of knowing exactly when her changelings were ready to change and these women were over ready for change. If she hadn't said anything they would still be sitting here every other Thursday getting nowhere fast, supporting each other as they slowly made the changes they wanted but bumping into many walls along the way.

'Keep working with your goals. The more clarity you have around them the quicker and easier it will be for you to achieve them. Now before we start today's session are you having your standard orders? Two lattes and a long black for Cynthia?'

'No I'm changing my order,' piped up Rebecca, 'I'll have a skinny soy latte. I can't expect to drop any weight if I don't change my order here.' Cynthia rolled her eyes good humouredly at Rebecca and Joy lifted her eyebrows in mock surprise at the change in Rebecca's order giving her the Princess glance she saved for especially difficult women. The girls knew it was not meant and took no offence. But they wondered how long Rebecca and her skinny soy latte would last.

'Sure you don't want it decaffeinated while you're at it?' dropped Cynthia into the mix.

Primly and intently Rebecca answered with a sweet no to end the conversation around her beverage of choice.

'For today's lesson,' started Joy, 'every one of you is unique and it is no use trying to be anyone but you. Your personality is pretty much fixed from a very early age and will direct the way you act and present yourself to the world. I want you to go home from here and until we catch up next look at how well you relate to your wardrobe. Does it describe the real you that you want to be or do you feel as if you are trying to be someone else?'

'You've lost me now Joy. I couldn't imagine being anyone but myself,' said Louise

'Exactly, is that our lesson to go home and look into our wardrobes? That doesn't make sense. Mine is filled with clothes. What else are you expecting to find?' questioned Louise.

'I am hoping to find you. And if I don't find you, I want to find a good reason why another person is hiding in your closet. Let me put it another way. Have you ever met someone and immediately got an impression on who they were only to discover that behind their clothing, or their image someone completely different was hiding? Many times we don't think about what we are wearing or how we look to those around us. Your clothes should reflect who you are. But the messages can get mixed. Come on why don't each of you describe to me why you chose what you are wearing today? As you started Louise let's start with you.'

Why me, thought Louise. Louise was just finding this day getting longer and harder as she sat there. *Why couldn't they go back to just having a coffee and pretending their lives were fine?*

Chapter 4.

Come out, come out wherever you are

Come out, come out wherever you are

Dinner. When had dinner been more than a pizza with the kids, or a quick bite at the local? Louise and Rob had never really gone out much and if Louise was honest with herself she was the main reason. It was not that she didn't like going out but the fuss and bother needed to go to the flash restaurants which Rob took her to for his work functions always bothered her. The girls all looked gloriously up at the men around them and down on her. No, that wasn't really true. They were all really nice but Louise just wasn't comfortable in heels. She had one 'going out' outfit. She had bought it seven years ago and it made it to every wedding and formal event they went to. She had realised it was coming to the end of its use-by as the groups were starting to cross over and she wasn't that dim to think she could wear the same dress again and again and again without repercussion. She still vividly remembered the girl at school who wore, or so it seemed, the same skirt and top to every casual dress day they had. Now Louise was no fashionista but her friends and especially Cynthia and Rebecca always looked fabulous and the comments they made behind that poor girl's back. She could still remember her name, Julie Waymar. Funny she couldn't remember some of the girls in her final year who were at the reunion all those months ago but Julie Waymar and she caught the train together for six years from Patterson to Mentone. Julie Waymar and her pleated skirt and white shirt with the Peter Pan collar and skinny velvet ribbon tied under the collar, long white socks and black Mary Jane shoes. The shoes were not so different to her school shoes only her school shoes were brown. When they were particularly evil the girls would snigger that she only had one pair of shoes and her parents painted them whatever colour they needed to be for each day.

Louise then started to describe to Joy and the girls her favourite going out outfit. She had bought it six months earlier. It consisted of a pair of chocolate trousers, her cream silk shirt with the brown collar and cuffs, her low wedge heeled suede boots and the amber earrings and pendant that Rob bought her for her last birthday. It was the amber earring that she always felt a million dollars in, unlike the rest of her jewellery. Which was surprising as she could not fault Rob on his generosity when it came to jewellery. She had bracelets and necklaces all filled with variations of precious and semi precious stones. For their 15th wedding anniversary he had bought her a one carat diamond pendant. She had it stored away in the safe. Pity it wouldn't bring in much if she hocked it. Anyway she still liked to wear it on family occasions as the kids were just as proud as Rob was when he presented it to her. It was just as much a gift from them as it was from him. The rest of her jewellery was nice, indeed some would say very nice, but wearing her jewellery made her nervous. Either the value, as with the carat diamond, or they felt too fragile and she believed she would break the pieces. Her fingers were not fine, in fact whilst she was not a full figured woman, she had a small frame with hands that no one would call delicate. Those hands could get down and dirty and that was just the way she loved to live life. So her delicate rings were dwarfed by her hands and the fine bracelets would end up getting caught on her clothing or looking lost on her wrist.

Describing her ideal clothing for the home was easy, let's see there were jeans with a shirt, pants with a shirt, oh and on a chilly winter's Sunday when she didn't leave the house there were her yoga pants with a long sleeved tee. She has lace-ups for walking in, ballet flats, but not the sort with decoration on them, more the original jiffy for moving around the house in and her favourite of all favourites, her beige suede loafers for going out to lunch in. Oh, look, she had them on again right now. With that realisation Louise put her foot out to the side of her chair to display her loafers that were under her navy trousers that she had on today. Today her shoulder length hair was dried straight with the top section pulled back together at the top of her head. Other days she might wear it in a low ponytail and she always had her fringe cut low on her forehead just above her eyebrows. Many thought she could pass for Sarah Palin during the last American election. Around her neck she had on the pastel pink and blue floral scarf that the kids had sent her for Christmas last year. Somehow she guessed Jade had chosen it and just told Paul to cough up the money. Her children were great but it was her daughter who resembled her most, while Paul had many of his father's tendencies. Here's hoping he is a bit better with his finances, she thought tiredly.

'Come on Louise back to us. Forget Rob and Paul for now. We are focusing on you. From the sound of things you pretty much wear pants all of the time?' asked Joy.

'You would think so and it sounded that way but Rob loved me wearing skirts and dresses so I have a few, which I just forgot to mention and a whole cupboard filled with pretty little sandals and flats to wear with them. I don't know why I forgot to mention them.'

Joy seemed to look at Louise knowingly and the girls held their breath as they expected to hear Joy's comments on what sounded like a completely logical selection of clothing from Louise and nothing really outstanding or unexpected. It was no surprise then when there was an audible sigh of relief from Louise when Joy turned her attention to look across the table at Rebecca and ask her the same question about her clothing and what she liked and did not like to wear.

Rebecca was not made of the same stuff as Louise. Her eyes lit up as she mentally walked through her wardrobe. Her favourite item? Let's see, well, that would have to be her blue silk dress which wraps around the body hugging her curves and edged in lace a deeper shade in midnight blue with a hint of shimmer through the edging. This she wore to a Christmas party four, maybe five years ago. It had a Grecian one shouldered neckline and came to just above her knees. Justin thought she looked like a Grecian goddess in it and she felt like a goddess but it did accentuate her hips just a little. It was a bit tight now but it was still in pride of place in the glamorous end of her wardrobe. She wore her tiny crystal chandelier earring with this dress and no necklace as the lace edging made her neckline busy enough and she carried that tiny pearl handbag she had had since her 20s. It was a little Oroton purse her mother gave her for her 21st. But hang on there. There was also the pearly pink sweetheart neckline dress, which flowed straight from the bust past her hips and gave her a stunning cleavage without packing on the pounds at her waist. Oh yes, she loved that dress and the delicate strappy heels with the tiny little flowers on the heel that she wore with it. She had a delicate necklace with enamelled flowers with crystal centres that seemed to flutter around her neck and a pair of matching stud earrings. She carried a long clutch with that dress that had a plain finish and a crystal closure. But then she couldn't go past her new pair of Prada shoes. They will last her a lifetime. They are gold and silver straps and the gold heel is encrusted with crystals in star shapes. That outfit is all about the shoes. Yes that would have to be her favourite, wearing those shoes with her simple black sheer shift. Black was not a bad colour on her and it did make her look thinner so it was a win-win situation all around with that dress. The fabric was sheer not the dress as there were some serious undergarments occurring with all of these outfits. Yes, she never went out without Nancy giving her a little hand.

'Nancy?' questioned Louise.

'Yes my Nancy Gantz pants or slip or tummy trimmer. Or for the big events there is my Nancy Gantz body trimmer. You will never find me out at night without a little Nancy holding me in place. Let's not forget with that dress I wear the single diamond pendant Justin gave me when Jacob was born and the matching earrings I got when Lucas was born.'

'Too bad you didn't have any more kids you would have been your own personal diamond mine.'

Rebecca blushed. She knew Justin spoiled her and why not, she was worth it and she did love diamonds. There was no pretending that Rebecca was not a girlie girl.

'Tell me Rebecca,' asked Joy, 'how many pairs of jeans do you have?'

Hmm, Rebecca had to think about that for a minute, 'only two, why?'

'And what about gym shoes or runners? We always see you in these ballet flats but rarely do I see you looking like you are going to get into the garden or go running after your boys.'

At this the girls laughed. Rebecca may have been a gym junkie before the boys were born and she would spend hours on the treadmill but she would always change on her way to and from the gym. She did have runners and sports shoes as she felt she should buy them to exercise in and they remained in their boxes at the back of her wardrobe. Rebecca's wardrobe was a sight to behold. Her shoes were all still in their boxes and she placed a picture of the shoes on the outside so that she knew exactly what was where. And the runners all stayed in the back of the cupboard these days.

'Is that important? Does it matter how many pairs of jeans or runners or heels any woman has, even if Justin swears that I am an incarnation of Imelda Marcos and her wild shoe fetish. I'm just like any girl that loves shoes.'

'Becs seriously you are the only girl any of us knows who has a wardrobe for her shoes and has them sorted by colour and heel height and season. Get real. You have more shoes that the local shoe store,' ribbed Louise. 'You give Cynthia a run for her money and that is tight but you win in the shoes stakes.'

'And your point is?' returned Becs earnestly. No one was going to tell her that she had too many shoes. Shoes were her lifeline and anyway your feet never look fat in shoes. Not unless they were too tight but that was a whole other issue. She knew the girls were only stirring her so she relaxed and joined in on the laughter.

'So is it my turn yet,' asked Cynthia, obviously keen to start talking about herself and her wardrobe. This really had been the quietest she had been in weeks, possibly even months.

'Go ahead Cynthia. Tell us about your wardrobe or what little there is of it.' Cynthia looked down at her short skirt and wondered was Joy saying she only had a few items in her wardrobe and if that was the case she had to go out shopping this very afternoon to correct that or was it a go at her short skirts. Winter was a great time of year. She could get away with wearing her skirts a bit shorter than summer as she had the excuse of wearing tights and that they compensated for the shortness of her skirts.

'I am going to ignore that remark. I am well covered.' Her manicured brows rose in mock astonishment at the women who sat with her and Cynthia settled into relating her wardrobe to all around her.

Cynthia was having the time of her life describing her favourite outfit. The only problem was she was not settling for one, it appeared to the women that she was happily describing her entire wardrobe. There was the wonderful cashmere mini dress she had purchased last season. This she wore with her Shooties.

'Shooties?' the women asked in unison.

'God, do you women have no style, why ever do I hang out with you?'

'We are your fortnightly dose of normalcy in your wildly exotic world but please explain what a shootie is or should we not ask.

Does it go over or under your clothing, and can you wear it in decent company?' More laughter followed as the women scrambled in their minds for what or who a shootie may be.

'They are a shoe for you fashionably ignorant bunch of slipper wearing sweeties.' The sweeties won them over or an all out brawl may have started around the corner table in Joy's café. 'I have them on today. They are a mixture between a shoe and a boot. They are fabulous in winter especially with long jumper dresses and thick winter tights.'

'Don't you mean jumpess's,' Rebecca asked and the girls started laughing again. Joy knew when it came to Cynthia and her wardrobe there was going to be loads of fun and laughter as there was nothing standard in her selection of clothing. So far the best way Joy felt to describe Cynthia's style was short, tight, extreme, erotic, seductive and explosive. How her breasts had managed to stay in that very low top she wore over summer was anyone's guess. Thank goodness she was only a B-cup. If Cynthia had Rebecca's breasts she would be exploding out of her tops at any given moment. But it was not as if Cynthia was cheap. She managed to straddle the thin line of dangerous without falling into the pit of whorish. It was never Cynthia's motive to look cheap, she just loved people noticing her and she loved fashion. She had a wardrobe of True Religion jeans because they looked amazing on her body. She was always in the QV Building or hunting through the shops at Melbourne Central to find something that little bit different. It would have been impossible to copy Cynthia's look, she knew her shape and she knew how to look amazing.

Returning to her description of her wardrobe Cynthia outlined what she would wear when she was relaxing at home, with a twinkle in her eye declared 'Chanel #5 Ladies and nothing else.' With that the girls all threw their napkins at her and she laughed unashamedly with them.

'Ok ladies, I think I've got the picture on each of you,' said Joy.

'You have?', they echoed as one.

'As I mentioned earlier the way you dress is an indication of who you are or it should be. We do judge a book by its cover, no matter what anyone says so if the cover of the book doesn't match the contents you feel let down or even cheated that you wasted your time and money on it. I wanted to hear about your wardrobe to get a feel for the type of person you are. What you like and don't like and if you are being true to yourself. I can tell you in front of me two out of three is not a bad result.'

'Two out of three what? Are right or are wrong?' asked Rebecca, who never for a moment doubted her own style so was very comfortable in asking the question. Cynthia never doubted her style either but hadn't even considered that might be an issue.

'Let me explain this to you,' started Joy. 'My mother was the A-typical Classical lady. Her skirts were never too tight or too lose. And Edith Head famously said "Your clothes should be tight enough to show you are a woman yet lose enough to show you are a lady". My mother was always the lady. Even though it was an era of propriety in all things she never wore lipstick, unless it she out and then it was only a light smudge of the most natural colour. She wore plain classic prints, tweeds, herringbone, stripes and checks. Her blouses may have had a light floral print to them but everything else was plain. She had her hat and gloves for every time we went into the city and wore sensible shoes with a small heel. And never, I repeat never, was she without hosiery once the war was over. My Mother was a lady and we treated her with the respect she deserved. You would never answer back to her and Mother never raised her voice to us. Now have a look at me. I am anything but Classic.'

The girls nodded their heads in agreement here. Joy was one of the most bohemian dressing women they had ever encountered. She seemed to have an endless array of summer and winter caftans and cassocks. Everything was loose and wispy around her body, the colours were eclectic and her earrings hung from her ears in a dazzling display of ethnicity without being overpowering. One moment her outfits seemed inspired by the sands of the Sahara and then next she would wear pieces of Victorian jewellery which would never have looked out of place on a school head mistress. From her long fob chains to her pince-nez perched precariously on the end of her nose.

Joy could see their confusion.

'Ladies, I am what you may call a Creative personality type. I love thinking outside the box. I cannot march to anyone else's drum and frankly I don't want to nor have I ever wished for the good graces of anyone else. I am who I am and no one can make me otherwise. My mother would tear her hair out with me continually hoping I would conform but it was never a part of my DNA. Once we all came to terms with that life was so much calmer at home. Luckily I was never in a position where I had to conform as mine is a tricky personality to place standards around and guidelines. You three girls are a different set of personality types altogether and to some degree you have not surprised me at all. While on the other hand there is one of you hiding yourself from the world.'

'Okay, okay, okay,' jumped in Cynthia, 'I get that all the time. I am not being true to myself. I am running around being someone else. Well you know what Joy. I like who I am. I like the way I dress. I am tired of people trying to tell me that I am hiding, that I am not revealing my inner being that I should express myself more. Look at this dress. How much more expression can one girl have!' That was true, Cynthia looked amazing in her dove grey and black fine knit dress with her charcoal grey patterned tights and her knee high patent black leather boots. Her make-up was expertly applied and her nails were well manicured and her nail polish was black. There was nothing subdued about her image whatsoever.

'Thank you Cynthia but I was not talking about you. You are very true to your personality type. You are without doubt a true blue Dramatic. There is nothing subdued or quiet about you. What you see is what you get, and at times that can be a bit too loud but it is true to your personality. If you don't mind I wouldn't mind turning your volume down a little when you are at work to get you that promotion you are after. Just tell me. Did you seriously go to work in that outfit this morning?'

'Sure why not?'

'Were you in any client meetings or hiding in your office all morning?'

'We had our team meetings and I met with my manager to discuss a potential new client we may be getting. They wanted them to go with John the new brownnoser in the office next to mine though.'

'Did you ask why?'

'Of course I did and they thought that I was not ready for this client. As if, I've been there for 14 months now and as yet am I to get my own clients.'

'Tell me about Asquith and Moore. What type of industry do they do recruitment for?'

'Well they have two levels, there is the admin/entry staff level at which I am currently working and the executive search level where I want to go.'

'So tell me why do you dress like you are going to lunch with the girls and not to work to fill an upper executive position?'

'But I am not looking for work in those positions just filling them.'

'That is where you are wrong. For someone to believe that you can fill that position you must first look like you belong and that you speak their language. At this stage you are not fitting the image they are after. Do me a favour. Think about how you expect your candidates to dress and dress on a similar parallel. By that I mean if you know that most of the clients are white collar traditionalist create a similar look yourself.'

'But that will be so boring. You can't be serious!'

'Wait a minute let me finish. I want you to still wear the same colours but opt for longer skirts, can you have them at least reaching your knees. Then try your shirts fitting a tad more modestly, super skin tight is not ideal and then you can go way out with your accessories so that we do not shut down your personality all together. When you are at work think of it as play time with dress ups and you have to play dressing up as a corporate highly successful executive. There has to be some women out there with some panache who you admire. Emulate them over the next month and let's see what happens. Okay?'

'Okay,' countered Cynthia.

'Now Rebecca, when was the last time you allowed yourself to look glamorous? My guess is you were something of a Jayne Mansfield in your day.'

'A Jayne Who?'

'Alright, bit before your time. I'm sorry. Gina Lollobrigida, Sophia Loren.'

'Joy, where are you pulling these names from? The Ark?'

'I think Joy means a Katy Perry or a Jennifer Lopez look. Sexy-womanly look. Is that right Joy, oozing sex appeal without being trashy?'

'Joy, chill, the last time I looked sexy Luke was conceived, give me a break. And my body is not what it used to be. I couldn't pull off that look any longer. I'm a mother now. What would the boys think if their mother was walking around with her girls up and proud?'

'Rebecca, I think it is time you started to realise that you are a fully Feminine woman. You love your frills and boys. You love everything about looking like a woman so get back to wearing your skirts, or your pretty little tops. You are not looking frumpy, as you never could, but the glamour has dimmed in you.'

'You try running around after two boys and your glamour would dim too.'

'Rebecca,' Joy said kindly, 'it is time to think about Justin. You have said that he loves you exactly the way you are and that is not at question here but do you?'

The corners of Rebecca's mouth twisted as she thought about Joy's words. Maybe she had lost her zip in the past few years. It wouldn't take a lot more effort to have her nails done again and it was time she got a great hair cut again and not just a trim to stop the split ends.

'So, Joy, what has my wardrobe description also told you about me?'

'Not much more than I didn't already know. You are a girlie girl. So don't fight it but stop wasting your money on runners and practical clothing. You will never be practical. It is just a waste of money. Buy new gym shoes when your old ones wear out. You may see the other mothers running around in yoga pants and gym shoes but it is not your personality. You are wasting your time, your precious wardrobe space and Justin's money. It is time to regain the woman within and let her free again.'

The conversation between Rebecca and Joy was closing and Louise knew her turn was next. There was a gnawing in her stomach. What was it that she was afraid of? She couldn't imagine Joy calling her a Dramatic like Cynthia, that wasn't her. Potentially she could be a Feminine like Rebecca, but there was no way she could go the sex kitten number. God help her if Joy told her she was wacky like her. What was it again? That's right Creative. More like mad if you asked her. Bohemian my toenail, she thought. It is just an excuse to put anything and everything together. That's it she though I must be a Classic like her mother. That would explain everything.

'So, Louise, the only personality we have to explore is yours.'

'That's okay. I think I have already figured myself out. I must be a Classic.'

'Nice try but no cigar I am afraid. You are a hidden Natural.'

'What?' Louise asked her head tilted to the side trying to understand Joy.

'A hidden Natural. I believe you have been all of your life but you have been too afraid to express yourself. Think about everything you said to me earlier. You LOVE the amber jewellery Rob gave you and only wore the diamonds because it gave other members of your family pleasure. You told me about all of your jeans and trousers and added the skirts and sandals as after thoughts. You are most at home in your garden, out walking, getting down and dirty. Even your artwork is nature based from what you say and your dream telescope will have you overlooking the ocean. More of nature. If you were a true Classic you would always have great shoes on your feet, pumps with your skirts and leather walking shoes with your trousers. You however love suede slip-ons, you detest high heels and will wear them only under duress. Wearing a suit would be like putting you in a straight jacket every day. You hide your true nature behind your feminine shoulder length hair. Have you considered cropping your hair? You would look amazing. And what is it with all of those pink jumpers and scarves you have?'

'Well my sister gave me the jumper and Rob and the kids used to buy me a new scarf every year.'

'Did you ever tell them you didn't like the scarves?'

'How could I? They were so pleased with themselves.'

'Let me guess your sister used to help them in the beginning. No Rebecca did.'

'Ah there is your answer.'

'Hang on a minute I was only trying to help. Don't blame this on me,' interjected Rebecca.

'It's okay Rebecca, nothing is your fault. You were never given any other indication of what Louise would like and we always choose something we would love ourselves if we are not clear on what the likes and dislikes are of the person we are shopping for.'

'But Louise was one of my best friends in school. Are you saying that I don't know Louise?'

'Not at all. I am saying that I don't think Louise knew Louise until now herself. Is that true Louise? Did you let Rebecca's style influence you?'

'It is so long ago now but Rebecca was always so gorgeous and I was so dorky that I loved her influence on my wardrobe. It made me feel like a woman. You try having hands like spades. Nothing about me was feminine. I had no boobs, no bum, no waist. I was as sexy as an ironing board. A touch of Rebecca made me feel a little like her.'

'That is so sweet Lou, but there was never anything wrong with you. I always admired how firm your body was while mine was all squishy.'

'I would have taken squishy any day.'

'Alright, back to Louise now. Louise, I think you are starting for the first time in a very long time to allow anyone to see the real you but you have to see you before others can too. Will you let me help you raise the curtain on your life and who you are?'

And there it was, the knot that was in Louise's stomach. The truth she had been hiding all of these years. She was not the elegant lady she had always invoked but a down to earth hippie, earth mother without the caftans and unwashed hair. However, the realisation didn't come with a clap of thunder and her friends shunning her from their midst. Their faces did not change their comprehension of how she had been hiding herself all of these years. The truth that she was a phoney didn't seem to disturb them at all. Maybe she was the only one she had been fooling all this time. The hammer didn't come down. No bolts of lightning exploded in the sky. She was the only doofus affected by her image. No one could care less but she had managed to hide her true self for almost 40 years. Well 38 to be exact. To them it did not alter anything and you know what. The knot was gone.

'Holy shit. What have I been doing all these years? Get these damn frills from around my neck.'

'You don't like that scarf?' asked Rebecca. 'Great hand it over Lou. I won't take any offence but will happily pick up any bits you no longer need as you have some great stuff at home.'

Louise handed over the scarf to Rebecca who eagerly wrapped the delicate confection of frills and a touch of lace around her own neck. Louise looked up at Joy, no longer afraid but questioning her next step.

'Joy what do I do now? I don't know what to look for or who I am? How do I begin?'

'Louise you are still the same down to earth woman you have always been. Can I make a few suggestions? They are a bit dramatic so hear me out. Your hair is nice. Now in this instance nice is a four letter word so I want you to go and get it cut. Wear the clothes that only you feel at home in. This is a great time for you with the kids away they can't influence you and, well, Rob is Rob and living his own life so you don't have to bother with his feelings. It is only you that you have to impress. But you must promise me when you go shopping that only something that you may think is a guilty pleasure can be looked at. In your case that guilty pleasure is the real you creeping out. We want her to burst forth and be forever centre stage. Can you do that for me?'

With a smile from ear to ear Louise nodded her head. There was a hint of a tear in the corner of her eye as she felt she had been seen for the first time in her life and it felt good.

'Okay ladies, that is enough for today's lesson. I want you to go home and look deeply into your wardrobes. Louise, start revealing the true you, Cynthia, try to stop revealing so much of you and Rebecca, start looking at yourself again. There is no harm in tossing out anything that does not suit your true personality. What you are on the inside we want reflected on the outside.'

Chapter 5.

Looking within

Looking within

Back at home Louise sat and thought about her life. Only nine months ago she had woken to that feeling of freedom that came with her children moving out and starting her new life with Rob only here he was now in Bali with Miss Masseuse and she alone in their old family home. The memories surrounded her with a comfort that warmed like a back rub on a winter's evening while at the same time stabbed at her heart relentlessly over all that was gone. Not lost as she deep down knew it really was only on loan to her. Her children were always going to leave home and well Rob had travelled so much that to find herself alone could have been her reality without all of the pain. It just didn't feel right. Maybe it was time to consider selling the house? Did she really need this huge house all to herself anyway? But what would the kids think? Paul may not be back for years so he shouldn't be a problem but Jade would be back during her school break and she would want her old room back surely. Maybe she could do some remodelling. After today's session at the Café Club with Joy, Louise was a little nervous over what direction she should take. Sure the knot was gone from her stomach but what was there in its place? There seemed to be a void. No, an abyss. A hollow nothingness that came from hiding her whole life behind everyone else's needs and desires. She had never knowingly lived her life trying to be everyone else. It was just easier to go with the flow and keep everyone happy. What was it Joy said about her style? Easy going? Now that really wasn't such a bad thing. Sitting here on the couch was getting her nowhere fast. The television was off and it was dark. So it was either time to go to bed or do something. She didn't have the money for remodelling so she could look for a job. It was evening and it was raining outside so job hunting could wait for tomorrow morning when she grabbed the paper. Too bad she had already tossed today's paper in the bin for the rubbish collection in the morning. She was starting to run out of ideas. She really couldn't go to bed at 7.30pm so what else was there? The thought of picking up a book did inspire her but her mind could not still after the revelations of the day. Well if I am going to discover my true inner self I suppose a great way to start is to rid myself of everything I don't like. That should narrow things down. Finally a plan evolved in her mind and the best place to start was in her wardrobe. This shouldn't take long she thought. Her wardrobe was not huge but she had managed to fill both cupboards since Rob had left. No longer were her tops crammed into drawers nor were her trousers piled up on the top shelf of her wardrobe stacked up on each other where those that had not been seen for a season had filtered to the bottom and the back of the pile. Every pair of trousers had their own hanger. This was decadent. Where to start? That was the problem. Well let's do this logically she thought. I'll look at this first hanger and work my way across the rack. An hour later found Louise having the time of her life. Some clothes were discarded with the flick of a wrist. They were thrown onto the growing pile at the foot of her bed. Others like a well worn mohair jumper from the 1980s was a prime example of what she believed Joy was referring to her style to be. However she was sure Joy would not be recommending she wear this ratty jumper out. But it did hold loving memories of winters when both kids were babies. This she would keep for days at home and days when she needed to remember life when it was full of family warmth. The olive green sateen skirt and with co-ordinating cream silk lace camisole was going out. Sure the colour may go with her eyes but the fabric felt as if she was walking with paper dolls clothing on. There was the constant rustling noise and the way it poked out at all angles when she sat down made her feel ridiculous. This was not one of her finer purchases. Just like all of those pink sweaters that Joy had described. They had become a staple in her everyday dressing, and considering Louise was not one to look at herself for too long in a mirror really did little for her. She had to wear that ghastly pink lipstick in the same shade to even make them bearable, when she bothered to think about it. Rebecca could have these. She would look adorable in those and do them the justice they deserved.

Now Louise felt rested and her mind was soothed. She had slain some of her demons and she rediscovered clothes that she had long forgotten hiding in the back of her wardrobe that had not even reappeared when she had her ritual spreading of her clothing from one to two wardrobes all those months ago.

The phone ringing disturbed her contented mood but was a welcome intrusion when she heard her daughter Jade on the other end of the phone. Jade was going to be passing through Melbourne with some friends on her way to New Zealand to enjoy some skiing during her term break. Jade explained that she had booked her flight a day earlier than the others so she could catch up with her Mum. Louise was excited to see her youngest and tell her all of the news about her Thursdays with Joy and the girls. There was a week till Jade arrived so Louise decided to embrace her newly discovered style and have her hair cut just as Joy had recommended before Jade arrived. Jade would be so impressed with her. She just knew it.

Thursday morning arrived and the sun was rising on the tarmac at Melbourne airport. It was very early and Jade had flown over on the red eye flight overnight from Perth. She would be tired so Louise planned for them to have a quiet morning at home, then go out for lunch in St Kilda to the Stokehouse, follow that with some shopping in and around St Kilda and South Melbourne and then home again for a good cooked meal. She was sure Jade would not be eating properly on her own. She was very excited to hear Jade's comments about her new 'do'. She had gone to her local hairdresser who tried desperately to talk her out of cutting her hair. He couldn't understand why Louise wouldn't be happy with the way he had been cutting her hair for years and at first thought it was an insult to his styling. Once she explained herself to him further and how she wanted something that was fuss free he exploded with possibilities and was as excited as she was to be part of her transformation. He couldn't wait to be the one to reveal the new Louise. Just like a hairdresser he loved the creativity and the idea of being solely responsible for her image. His cut was fantastic. They didn't quite go straight to a short cropped look as both felt it would be moving too fast too soon for her but her agreed to slowly work with her as she felt more confident. He had cut more layers into her hair and shortened it considerably. There would be no more ponytails for Louise and her blunt fringe had also been chipped into to give her a more playful laid back look. Great she thought. I look more my age rather than an aging 20 something. She had put on her amber earrings and a chunky winter white jumper over her jeans. The overall look was polished yet easy going. Just her style. She did however put on her bracelet that the kids had bought her even though it didn't really go with her new look anymore. Maybe she should save this for evening functions she thought.

Jade's plane was 20 minutes late, typical for the domestic airlines these days and a very tired Jade walked off about amongst a sea of other tired travellers. Louise stood back waiting to see Jade's response to her look and was surprised when Jade walked by not noticing her.

'Jadey,' called Louise. At the sound of her name Jade swung around and her jaw dropped.

'Mum? What the hell have you done to yourself?' Louise had not expected this reaction from her youngest. This was the sort of reaction she would have expected from Paul or his father but not Jade, who interestingly had a very similar hair style to her Mother's now.

'That's a nice hello for your mother.' Louise stepped back and held her daughter at arms length, smiling at her the smile only a mother can bestow on her child.

'I'm sorry Mum but you surprised me. What's with the new look. You look ... different.'

'Different good or different bad?' Louise cocked her head to the side, not too sure if she was happy or not with Jade's comment.

'I don't know just different. Has Dad seen you like this?'

'What has your father got to do with this? In case you forgot he left me and is holidaying in Bali with his new girlfriend as we speak. And don't start me on where they got the money.'

'I'm sorry. Wow you look great but ... different that's all.' With those words they walked silently to the baggage claim area each lost in their own world. Louise wondered if she had made a mistake. Her hair could grow back and if she blow dried it when she got home she could probably get a sleeker finish to the ends. Maybe she should have put a bit more make-up on to meet Jade. There was no need to completely freak her out. Jade was having her own thoughts. For the first time in her life she saw her Mum as a woman. Not just her Mum and it unnerved her a little. When Louise had thought that Jade would be the easiest to turn around she was actually going to be the hardest. Being the baby she liked things to stay as they were. Nothing had every really changed in her life unless she made the change. It was hard enough coming to terms with her parents separating but now her Mum was transforming into someone she didn't know. This was going to take some getting used to.

The rest of the day was fun and by evening as they were putting the dishes away Jade came up to her Mum and placed her hands on her shoulders.

'You know Mum; I know you changed your hair when you got home because of me. You really shouldn't have. I quite like this new you. And from the sound of what you are doing with your girlfriends that is a great thing for you. It is time you stepped out of the family shadow. But can you do me one favour. Can you not look better than me when we next catch up? I'll have to start telling people you're my friend and not my daggy old Mum any more.' It truly was a hallmark moment as Louise hugged her youngest. She hadn't even thought how her moving on with her life would affect those around her. This moment was precious and who cared if she wore diamonds in the daytime. They were her diamonds after all.

Rebecca had a much easier time with her transition at home. Justin loved the fact that his wife was sexing herself up again. Not that Rebecca was exposing cleavage and dressing like Cynthia but she was taking a few more minutes in the morning to do her hair and she had changed her clear lip-gloss for one with a light pink tint. She had gone out and bought some more fitted tops to wear over her pants and had even had her nails done again after too many years of not bothering. She felt like a woman again. Even one of the mothers at school pick up had asked her if she had lost weight. Yeah! She may have lost half a kilo by cutting out the extra sugar in her coffee but the simple act of wearing clothing that fitted her made her appear slimmer to them. To her she felt as if she was exposing her size more and felt larger but the truth was that by hiding herself for so long they all assumed that she was much larger than she truly was.

Over the weekend when she went to watch the boys play football she had thrown out all of her football clothing, the chunky scarves and the heavy knits because she never felt at home in them. She bought herself a gorgeous pale pink wool coat, and teamed it with some leather gloves in raspberry and a white turtleneck. Justin thought she looked as delicious as dessert and grabbed her around the waist playfully while she was trying to remain composed and intent on how well her boys were playing. Truth be known she still had no idea about the game but no one needed to know that. Justin loved her, her boys loved her and she felt whole again.

Cynthia's week fell somewhere between the two. She understood what Joy was telling her but her budget just did not allow for her to spend any more money right now. She was in a dilemma. She was simply going to have to be creative with what she already had.

Let's see she could wear her dresses as long tops over a pair of skinny leg pants. That would cover that problem. She had a drawer full of tank tops and coloured camisoles. These would work as layering pieces under her tighter top so that she didn't have to button them all the way up and could create some colour and sensibility and there was that fabulous Versace suit she had bought a couple of years ago. It was classically tailored, well as classical as Cynthia could be and wouldn't raise eyebrows surely if she wore it with some interesting shirts. She also had a stock of white shirts with French cuffed sleeves. All she needed to do was go out and grab some new cufflinks. The red lip cufflinks would probably be a no-no and the diamante encrusted squares and hearts would be a bit much for the office. She would just have to save her strappy shoes for after hours and her killer heels could hide under her suit pants. As she surveyed what she had she decided just to see how life treated her if she altered her look at work.

Monday was her first attempt with her new look. No one really said much at work as they took this to be one of Cynthia's phases and would only last a day. She did notice however that the guy she had seen at the bar a few weeks ago was waiting in reception when she walked through. How lucky was that, she thought, that she hadn't tried to pick him up on that night and gone home with him. He looked at her strangely as she passed him by. Please tell me that I didn't do anything to embarrass myself. She thought back quickly to the evening and could only remember having a few red wines and chatting to her girlfriend Lia that she was out with. No she was safe. She hadn't embarrassed herself. This time. After a week of wearing her 'new look' whispers were moving through the office. It was said that Louise was looking for a new job. Caught up in the intrigue was her supervisor Lyn, who called Cynthia into her office on Friday afternoon.

'So how's your work going Cynthia?'

'Good Lyn, nothing a new challenge couldn't improve though.'

'So it's true. You are planning on leaving us.'

'Whatever gave you that idea,' gasped Cynthia

'Gossip, you know this office. I was just checking. We hear so much around the office and I prefer to go straight to the source. Glad to hear you're not planning on going anywhere.'

'No I am not planning on going anywhere.'

'Good to hear. We'd miss you here. Oh and Cynthia.'

'Yeah?'

'You look good.'

Cynthia held her head high as she walked out. It was working. She hadn't expected to get a promotion straight away but in under a week people were noticing. Shit, Joy really knew her stuff. The excitement of this realisation had to be celebrated. Cynthia found out all of the girls from work were going out for a drink or two. She was looking forward to joining them and having a fun night out. She was going to go home and change but rather decided against it. She wondered would this new 'look' have the same impact on her sex life. She seriously hoped so.

The bar was pumping when she got there and she was able to find her friends easily in the crowd. There he was again. That guy from the reception area this morning. This was three times now that she had run into him, well been in the same vicinity as him and she felt it was kismet. Making the excuse of having to go to the bathroom she walked his way and pretended to be looking for someone as she did right over his shoulder so that accidentally they would lock eyes. Bingo, it worked. Men really could be so easy to pick up these days. She flashed him a smile and dropped her eyes to see if he would still be looking at her as she raised them again. And bingo again he was. As she came up to him her smiled genuinely warmed up her face. He was gorgeous after all.

Cynthia turned into the deep timbre of his voice before she even started listening to the words he was saying. Luckily she realised that he was addressing her.

'Haven't I seen you somewhere before? You look familiar to me?'

'No I don't think so.' *How could he not remember her? Play this one easy* she told herself. *Pretend to be thinking, smile and* 'I remember. I saw you earlier this week in the reception area at Asquith and Moore. I work there. Are you looking for work?'

'Not exactly. I was in there registering for job placement. I have returned this month from working in America for ten years. I stupidly decided to take a year off and now I'm finding it hard to get things started. I should have taken the job the American company offered me in Idaho and come home later when I had everything organised. Excuse my manners, hi, I'm Mike.'

'Cynthia, nice to meet you. What sort of work are you looking for?'

'Computer analyst and you. What do you do?'

'How's it going? Have they found you anything yet?'

'Yes, I've had a few interviews so it isn't as bleak as I had first thought but it isn't happening as quickly as I had initially thought. This will be the third agency I have gone to since I returned.'

'Well you have come to the right place. We are one of the biggest and the best.' After an hour of casual conversation Cynthia found herself not even returning to her friends. They were completely used to Cynthia going out and hooking up with someone. This was not to be one of those nights though.

'Cynthia, it was great to meet you but I am afraid I have to go. See you later.' And with that Mike left. Cynthia felt a little like a reverse Cinderella, only her prince left the ball at midnight. Mike had bought her two glasses of wine so not a complete loss and look who just walked in. Phil. They hadn't seen each other for a few months and he was fun. Phil joined Cynthia with her girlfriends and a very long very fun night was had by the group with Cynthia merrily jumping into a cab with Phil to take them to Chasers to go dancing then back to his house for the night. Oh well, in for a penny in for a pound she thought to herself.

Chapter 6.

Raise your glass

Raise your glass

Thursdays with Joy had become an escape for the girls. They never knew what Joy would have in mind for them or what new insights into their own lives they would reveal. And this Thursday was no different. The atmosphere of the Café Club was more evocative than normal. The lighting was subdued and the music more mellow. Generally on Thursday's Joy would have the lights bright, the music pumping and there was a festive feeling to this end of the week. Luckily for the girls the crowd did not appear until after the work day so they generally had the café to themselves between 1pm and 3pm. This week the mood was set for something different. In normal circumstances the girls would arrive separately and even though today they drove their own cars there they arrived within minutes of each other. Their entrances were unmistakable. From a distance the clatter of the Cynthia's heels was recognisable, just as the bubble of Rebecca's laugh carried through the air in the intensity of Louise's voice as she shared a joke with the girls. It was their time together, their time with Joy and they were all feeling that there was something different in store for them today.

The layout of the café had not changed but their table at the end of the bar was set as if for a party. On the table there were some crudités and dips, a glass of red wine, a glass of champagne and a martini glass. This idea tickled Louise's fancy as it was never too early in the day for her to have a drink. It did however take Rebecca back a heartbeat as she remembered her glory days before the boys when it was nothing to meet with her girlfriends at the Stokehouse in St Kilda or the Imperial on Chapel Street for a long lunch midweek. Every day was a day off for someone in the airlines and they didn't need an excuse to go out. It was a weekly occurrence. Many times they did not even make it back home after lunch, they just stayed put and partied into the evening. Luckily they all lived around the area so cabs were an easy option to get home and they could walk or ride to pick up their cars the next day. Louise raised her eyebrows to the set-up. She was partial to her afternoon latte and the idea of drinking mid week before 6pm was quite foreign. While everyone else was going out for midweek lunches Louise would have been home with her children or happily pottering in her garden.

She didn't mind the Saturday or Sunday long lunch but she had already had lunch and they were also studying of sorts. Weren't they? She was still waiting to hear everyone's thoughts on her new do and was surprised that no one had said anything just yet. It didn't take long though for the laughter to die down from her last joke and Cynthia to turn her cool gaze over Louise's fresh hair cut.

'Louise, have you done something different with your shoes today?'

Louise looked immediately at her feet in confusion only to hear Cynthia roar with her distinctive laughter whilst looking warmly at her.

'Lou, your hair looks fabulous. Whoever cut it is a genius. You look a good ten, no fifteen years younger. Joy you are amazing. How did you know Lou would look so good with short hair? How do you feel? I bet you feel fabulous too. Be careful, Lou you'll have the boys coming from everywhere when they hear that you are available and on the scene. That's it, I want you coming out with me this weekend. I know so many great guys; we'll hook you up for sure.'

By this point Lou was crimson. She did love her cut but the thought of hitting the town with Cynthia was more than she was ready for at this point. She was still rediscovering who she was without laying herself bare to strangers. As she recovered her composure Rebecca came to the rescue.

'Cyn you are incredible, give her a break, you hardly came up for air and we haven't heard from Lou yet how she feels. But can I say from the look on her face as she was walking towards me down the street she is very happy with herself. I don't think I have ever seen you look so refreshed. Anyway Cyn, if you know so many great men why aren't you dating any of them? Let me guess you are still dragging around with architect boy, what was his name? Hmm, that's right, Phil wasn't it? Forget her Lou, but do tell us how you feel and what did Jade say when she popped through the other night? I bet she loved it!'

As soon as the conversation was directed away from her personally and onto Jade, Louise was able to get her breath back and rejoin the conversation. She smiled to herself as she thought of the short visit she had with Jade only last weekend. There was no point bringing up the fact that Jade was less than enthusiastic with her look when she first saw her. It was Joy though who saw through her.

'So Louise tell us exactly what Jade thought of your look when she first saw you. No sugar coating now. Was she happy or was she surprised and off guard?'

Being asked if Jade was surprised was unexpected to Louise and her non poker playing face gave it all away. The quick down turn of her lips and the shift of her eyes quickly to the side were all that the girls needed. Rebecca afraid of what Cynthia may blurt out jumped in first.

'Don't tell us she didn't like it? You look great and she has such a wonderful sense of style too.'

'I think Jade was just surprised that Mum was no longer playing stay at home mum and that I was moving on from her father. She loved it in the end. It was just a shock to her that was all.' Now that she had started talking it was easy to go on. Louise hated to say anything bad about her kids or her life but the worst of it was out on the table now so there was no harm in continuing.

'Can you believe the first thing she asked me was what Rob thought of it? As if he has anything to do with it and I think my short response to that question was enough to let her know that the ways of the past are gone and it is a whole new world for us. Well for me at least. Her life all new and different. They have such a great life now these kids, travelling and studying. I don't regret my kids for an instant but I now see just how much living I gave up for them earlier on and I don't want to give up any more. I'll never be as sexy as you are Cyn, that's just not me but I don't have to be mumsy any more. I'm taking this one frightening step at a time because this really isn't easy for me. It has been easy staying as a mum but now that the kids and Rob don't need me it is exciting to see just who has been hiding in this shell all of this time.'

'Hear, hear, Louise, this is what I have been waiting for. Good girl. So Rebecca how was your fortnight? You look a little different today. Tell us about what has happened to you?'

Rebecca was pleased Joy had noticed. It had been fun taking care of herself again. Having her nails done was a great start to getting her old self back and even today she stopped at the shops on her way to meet the girls and had picked up a new top. It was just a top from Target but it felt good to spend some money on herself again after focusing on the boys for so long. She had even blow waved her hair. She was starting to feel like a woman and a vital woman at that.

'Not that the boys have noticed the change but the school mums stopped me the other morning and asked if I had been away. Can you believe it? All it took was a touch of lipstick, a splash of nail polish and a brush through my hair and they thought I had been on holidays. My God, how tired must I have been looking if that is all it took?'

Joy looked upon her favourite errant child in Cynthia. 'Cynthia, has there been any news from your side of the world. Have you climbed that corporate ladder any higher since we last caught up?'

'There have been no changes as such but I did get called into the office by my boss wanting to quell any rumours I was planning to leave. All I had done was start dressing a bit more demurely and they thought I had another job to go to. Something odd did happen though. Do you remember that bloke I saw out a few months ago? Well I saw him in at the office and then out on Friday night last week. I swear he was into me. We talked and hung out for most of the night and then without a word he said he had to go and was gone. No, can I get your number, shall we catch up again or anything. Just nice to see you and bye. What do you reckon that was all about?'

'He's got a girlfriend for sure,' suggested Rebecca.

'Or a wife and a brood of six children at home most probably. Or else he was waiting for someone else and they showed up so he left. Did you see anyone else come in?' offered Louise.

Cynthia thought back to Friday night, whilst Phil featured prominently in the late night recollections it was the time she spent with Mike that left her with a warm feeling. The way he left so suddenly baffled her. There had to be someone else so she figured it was best to forget him and focus on the here and now. Right in front of her were some tantalising glasses and they were now uppermost in her mind.

'Okay Joy, what gives with the drinks? Are we doing a tasting this afternoon? You know we don't usually start drinking so early but I'm always happy for a little afternoon aperitif and if the drinks are on you let's get into it.' With that Cynthia picked up the martini glass in front of her and prepared to clink glasses with the others until Joy's hrrmph from the bar made her pause and place her glass down.

'Yes there are some drinks out here today but they represent more than a celebratory toast. Each glass represents each of you and as I didn't want to miss out this time there is one for me as well.' With that the girls noticed that Joy had a margarita on the bench in front of her.

'This week we are going to be looking at your individual shapes and how you dress them. Have you noticed that each of you has a shape different to each other? I want you to understand and come to love your shape. It is unique and special to you. The more you understand how your shape works the less stress you will have when you are shopping and finding clothes to suit you.'

'So what's with the drinks then Joy?' asked Cynthia. 'Shouldn't you have a bowl of fruit out here so we can decide who is the pear, the orange, the apple and the banana or however it goes?'

'That is one way of looking at body shapes but when you work behind a bar everyday you start to see shapes in everything and I discovered that you are each a body shape that relates to each of the glasses in front of you. Each of you love to have a sip or in your case Cynthia a slurp of what each of those glasses contain and you find enjoyment within. However many women cringe at the thought of being called a pear shape. It is like an insult to who they are. And we all know what happens to fruit that is not fresh – it goes soft and mouldy.'

'Just like me,' moaned Rebecca.

'There is nothing mouldy about you Rebecca,' returned Joy. 'But let's start with Louise first. Louise you have in front of you a glass of champagne. It is straight up and down to allow the bubbles to travel up the glass. It consists of straight lines. Historically the champagne glass was the shape my William said I was. Remember it has a very wide bowl up high and a long stem. When I was younger I too had a very wide bust and absolutely no waist or hips to speak of. Over time though the champagne glass changed and it is now a lovely long flute. It is bubbly and allows the champagne to be effervescent and tickle the nose. When I look at you Louise I see the champagne flute. Your shape will always be happiest in straighter lines. Trousers and well cut shirts. If you wear a dress you will suit a shirtmaker or a simple shift. You have almost no waist which is a designers dream. You may think you look boyish but have you had a look at those girls on the runways?

Most of them are coat hangers with legs. Straight up and down. You need to look at clothing that reflects the straight lines in your body. Avoid anything which is heavily shaped in at your waist as it won't sit properly. Just as any tops that are cross over will make your bust disappear. You only have a small bust so wear a higher neck top, which luckily suits your personality and will give you more shape. You will suit anything with a belt or if you want the appearance of more curves wear crisper fabrics which will hold their shape. Thin floaty fabrics on you will hang limp and accentuate the fact that you have no shape. How does that fit with your idea of how you dress?'

Louise looked at the girls and then back to Joy.

'I've got two thoughts here. You have just explained why so many crossover dresses look stupid on me. I wanted that curvy woman's shape and I ended up looking like an ironing board. Especially when I tried on the wrap style dresses that were so big over the last couple of years and why cross over tops sagged at my bust unless I tied them very tight and then I couldn't breathe. But I have to ask you Joy. You mentioned something I don't know You will have to excuse my ignorance but what is a shirtmaker dress? It sounds like a big shirt.'

'That dear girl is exactly what it is. The shirtmaker style is buttoned through to the skirt and has a belted waist. With your shape you will look fabulous. Make sure it fits you immaculately and you will turn heads in it.'

'I was glad to hear pants are my thing or I could really have been in trouble if I had to get rid of half of my wardrobe, no actually two thirds.'

'Structured clothing will look great on you and your champagne shape. Let's get those bubbles inside you bubbling up and not floating out into the wind in the wrong clothing.'

Louise liked the sound of that and was happy with the description of her shape. She smiled to herself picturing all of the floaty tops up in her wardrobe which she had always hated and now had a reason to throw out. Now she knew they didn't suit her personality and they were wrong for her shape. Oh dear, she thought, she had cleared out her cupboards last weekend it looked like another culling was around the corner. This is fun, she decided.

Cynthia nibbled on one of the crackers in front of her. Dying to take a drink but she knew it was improper to drink before she knew if that was actually her drink. She was pretty sure the dirty martini in front of her would be hers but she must wait and wait she would.

'Now to you Miss Cynthia. Do you recognise yourself in the glass in front of you?'

'Are you calling me a dirty martini? Cause I hope not. But I don't mind the thought of being shaken not stirred. Now that reminds me of something Phil tried on Friday night but I don't think you girls need the gory details.' If the girls were not with Joy they were sure they would have pelted Cynthia with mixed nuts but they knew then Joy would only have extra work to do cleaning up so they rolled their eyes and focused back on Joy in silent acknowledgment for her to continue.

'Cynthia I thought you were out with Mike Friday night? Isn't that what you told us before? Now I'm getting confused and I know I'm not that old.'

'I went out with the girls from work and ran into Mike in the city but then when Mike left Phil showed up so we spent the night and most of Saturday together. I know he's not The One for me but at least he is something for now. Better to lie in warm arms than a cold bed.'

'Cynthia you have to put a greater value on yourself, but we will get to that. I may have to bring that session with you girls forward. I hope though, as you start rediscovering the wondrous gifts within each of you, that your sense of value and worth will rise as well. We'll see what the coming months bring, but back to you now and the martini glass.'

Cynthia didn't feel rebuffed by Joy, she knew Phil was just a stand in but she didn't really see what was wrong with a casual fling. Anyway things were so much different these days weren't they to when Joy was her age. Upon reflection Joy would have been her age in the late 70s and those were pretty wild times too. She started to imagine Joy with her William and her long blonde hair, held in place with a scarf tied long at the side of her neck, large hoop earrings, a mini skirt or a maxi dress and high boots with a stacked heel. Cynthia could almost see herself living then as well. It wasn't so long ago really. But then Joy had her William and wouldn't have ever had a cold bed to go home to. A large part of Cynthia wanted that consistency of someone to love her and hold her every night. No matter what she said aloud, within she knew she was still looking for her happy ever after. She knew it was not with Phil but she felt better having at least happy for now and worry about the ever after later..

'Tell me Cynthia, what do you see when you look at that glass?'

'A very yummy, very naughty martini with two olives hanging over the side.'

'You're not looking at the glass. You are looking inside the glass. Look again.'

'Alright then I see a long stem and a wide sharp top. Sort of a V shape. Is that what you mean?' Cynthia was still interested as she knew this was about her but at the same time salivating for that drink, or at least one of the olives.

'Spot on. Well done. Go ahead have a sip while I describe your shape to you.' At this point Cynthia didn't need to be told twice, she quickly nibbled one of the olives and had a light sip of her drink as a small sigh escaped her lips and she relaxed back into her seat. Anyone at another table would have thought she was either an alcoholic ready for her fix or this was the most amazing cocktail ever served. Truth be known she was just enjoying the dramatics of the moment.

'Quick question for you Joy before we go on,' said Louise.

'Sure go ahead.'

'Why do you call it a dirty martini? I've heard that term but I don't know what it means. Cynthia certainly seems to like it but I don't know if I could drink anything called dirty.'

'Not a problem. The term dirty refers to the fact that I have added some olive juice from the jar of olives into the glass. Not just the olives. It gives it a saltier taste.'

'Try some,' said Cynthia.

'No that's fine I'm enjoying my bubbles here. Anyway back to you Joy. What were you saying about Cynthia?'

'Now that I have your attention again, Cynthia's body is reminiscent of the martini glass. Cynthia, you have the strong shoulders of a swimmer, with a small waist and small hips.'

'I bet you find it difficult to find clothing that fits you which is why you often resort to your more ostentatious styles as they are the looks you find work for you. You would have problems wearing a standard jacket well as to have it fit your shoulders you will find it is too big at the waist and rather than hiding your shape you will select shorter jackets that are cropped at the waist. The cropped jacket plays up the smallness of your waist and hips and makes you appear sexier than you may have intended. Another problem you will have is finding dresses, for the same reason, but you will find your way around this with strapless and or halter neck styles. You really will look best in separates and if you can create some fullness around your knees by way of kick pleats or frills you will balance out your shoulders and highlight your waist. Clothing will need to be tailored for you but try and soften your fit. You can get away with a very crisp finish but it can be too intimidating and this will not help you get ahead at work. You need a touch of softness in either your colours with a crisp finish, or a soft finish in the crisp colours you so love. By doing both you will be too intimidating for a consultant's role. Tone it down so that you can move on up.'

'I had never thought of it that way but you are right about why I always wear short jackets. I cannot stand how a jacket that will cover my shoulders hangs everywhere else. I lose all shape. '

'Get yourself a good tailor. If a jacket fits you in the shoulders it is amazing at what they can do for the rest of the jacket. The shoulders are the most important fit point on any jacket. If that is not right, nothing can be done with the rest. And a well fitting suit is not only super smart but makes a woman look incredibly professional.'

'Okay I get that, but didn't you say earlier that William said you were a champagne glass until they changed shape because we both have small waists and hips. Does that mean you are also a martini glass? Now I mean no offence but we are very different shapes now. Your shoulder line is a lot softer and I really couldn't see you in a crisp jacket.'

'Well picked up and I like the way you reference my shoulder line being soft. You pick these things up quickly. Whilst it is true I have small waist and hips like yours I have a very large bust and small shoulders. You have large shoulders and a small bust. This will create a huge difference. Today I am more of a margarita glass. Well rounded on the top and narrow on the bottom. You might say I am an older Pamela Anderson. We can dress similarly on the bottom half with clothing made up of crisp lines but when I was younger I loved to flaunt my bust. William loved Dolly Parton and I think he thought he had found a little of Dolly in me. God I used to love it when the two of us would sit in our car singing the old Kenny Rogers and Dolly Parton songs. Truth be known I thought she was pretty special too. Did I tell you once how we met her in Hawaii when we were there on holidays sometime in the mid 70s. William had a knack of bumping in to all sorts of people when we were travelling and next thing we knew we were having dinner with her and her husband on the terrace of our hotel room. Oh she was huge in country music back then but hadn't made any of the mainstream songs you would know her for today. I remember later that year she released "Here You Come Again". We never saw her again but I did get a lovely card from her when William died.'

The girls sat stunned. They knew that Joy and William had an amazing life together but the fullness of it was only starting to sink in. The loved to listen when Joy started talking about her past as but often averted the conversation away from herself and back to them as she did in this case again.

'Anyway as I was saying. Yes Cynthia there is a similarity in our shapes but mine is softer on top so I suit clothing that flows with the softened lines of my body as opposed to sharp lines that will not move with my body. You will notice that is why I am always in layers, it is partly my personality but also I am working with the line of my body. If I wore a crisp jacket I would look like the Michelin man's sister.'

Up till this point Rebecca had listened with interest as Joy described her girlfriends and their enviable body shapes, champagnes, martinis, what did that leave her with. Sitting in front of her was a fat glass of red wine. Typical. True she loved red wine but surely she was not going to be described as a goblet.

'Rebecca my dear that leaves you and you have the most delicious shape of all.'

'Yeah sure, bring out the brandy balloon, why don't you?'

'No my dear you are way too tall for that. That would have to be someone like Danny deVito. Rebecca you are like a wonderful Cabernet.

Rich and full bodied. The glass which holds the red wine is full in the bowl. You want to savour a good red wine as it fills the palate and comes in a beautiful array of rich flavours. The red wine glass has no waist but is designed to allow the wine to breathe and be savoured at its best.' When it was put like that it didn't sound so bad after all.

'Rebecca, you have a gorgeous shape, you are full of curves and a richness of shape. Just as in the red wine glass and who doesn't love a full bodied luscious red wine. Songs have been sung to your shape. Think Red Red Wine. When I first heard it, it was sung by Neil Diamond but you will probably know the UB40 version. What you have to stop doing is trying to show off your waist for the moment. I know you had a lovely waist and it will come back but until there is a narrowness there to your body you will look best in clothing that goes straight through. When you wear your pants wear your tops just over your waist. Even give pants a miss and slip into wrap dresses. There are gorgeous ones out there for winter that you can wear with patterned tights and low heeled boots and summer ones you can wear with your sandals. Wraps in soft colours will create movement and prettiness around your face or longer line jackets that go down to mid thigh will look wonderful on you. If you look around my bar you will also see my cocktail glasses, this is where you have come from and from the changes you are making it is where you are very likely to go back to. You are losing yourself in those baggy tops you were wearing. You think it hides your weight but what it does is it hides everything. If you don't want to wear dresses okay, although for the life of me I can't understand why as you have the most delightful figure, then look for some a-line skirts to swirl and swish in.'

'Are you sure I couldn't be a Sauv Blanc? The white wine glasses are smaller and not so bottom heavy.'

'Well you could be but generally I liken those girls with a fuller bottom and smaller bust there. And you definitely do not have a small bust. Don't worry. With the changes I can see already in your shape you will have that wasp like waist back in no time. You just had to start thinking about yourself again. That was all.'

'Wasp, bumblebee. I'll just be happy with a waist.'

'So ladies,' interrupted Joy, 'raise your glasses and let's drink a toast to your shape.'

Chapter 7.

I'm sorry. It's not you

I'm sorry. It's not you

The weekends were a delight to Louise. Whether the kids were around or not she spent these days in her garden looking after her plants. Lately they had had more tender loving care than usual and with the winter coming to an end it was time to prepare her garden for the spring time. She did not understand why it wasn't giving her the same level of contentment and satisfaction that it had? Of course her garden beds were well fertilised. There was not a weed in sight and her Spring bulbs were doing their best to start poking their heads through the soil. She should have been proud of the lushness of her lawn. Louise had been recycling water long before the government had issued the warnings about how low the catchments were. She had had two tanks put in up the side of her house two years earlier. She saved the grey water from her laundry and kept buckets in her kitchen and shower. Everyone thought she was being excessive in the early days but now they could see the difference because in her case her lawn was green all summer long and no one could accuse her of watering through the night or having underground watering systems. The whole neighbourhood had seen her at one time or another wandering around with her buckets and she proudly had her 'grey water used here' sign hanging from her front fence.

Louise was not seeing the beauty in her garden. She was feeling the absence of the ocean and the salt air in her lungs as she never had before. Growing up on Port Phillip Bay meant Louise had spent many summers lying on the beach at Mentone or taking the train and even occasionally hitch-hiking down to Portsea and Sorrento. Those were the days. She remembered in particular the summer before Rob. She was fifteen and she and Cynthia and Rebecca were enjoying their last innocent summer of fun. The girls had boyfriends but went no further than the odd pash in the cinemas. Holding hands was standard and if they really liked the boy they would let him feel their breasts but everything else was completely out of bounds. They knew about sex but were not interested in it just yet. They had all agreed to wait until they were sixteen. It was not uncommon to find all three girls out with their respective boyfriends sitting at someone's house on a Friday night with the telly going and not a lot of talking happening. It helped that generally their boyfriends all knew each other as well. That way everyone was happy and no one had to be alone. They always knew they would be friends for life but they had thought that they would all marry friends and be together all the time. They used to attend Yacht Club dances further down the coast at Mornington and Mt Martha when Rebecca was going out with Andrew. Often they spent more time outside the dance than inside the dance. Then there were the days spent lying on Mentone beach just down from the Life Saving Club. None of them were life savers but they knew lots of boys who were and it wasn't uncommon to hear one of the boys telling a new girl on the beach about the new taps that had been installed and did they want to see them. As soon as the girls heard this line they would cringe with embarrassment as there was nothing original in the boys trying to get a girl into the first aid room to make out. Summers were endless back then. Sunscreen was a waste of time and they would lie in the sun all day every day smearing their bodies with coconut oil that started the day solid in a screw top jar and melted with the heat of the day. Rebecca had found a great pattern for cotton bikinis and would sew each of them new bathers every week. Louise was almost one of the boys back then. She was never at a loss for words and when the surf was up she was into the waves a fast as any of them. Rebecca was happier sitting on the beach tanning. Waves had never excited her. Louise started thinking when the last time anything had excited her. Of course her kids and their achievement made her proud but her she was looking at her garden and there was a numbness to her. She wanted to feel the exhilaration again that running into the waves on a cold summer's day could do to you. Plunging head first into waves five foot high and body surfing back into shore. Then dashing up the beach when you were finished feeling as if the blood would never flow to your toes or fingers again. She never saw any of those boys any more. Most of them went to the brother school and she had lost touch years before. If anyone knew where to find them Cynthia would. She was the most socialiable of all of the girls or Rebecca as she was still in the area. When Rob had suggested that they move to Balwyn it had sounded so grown up. They had a pool in the back yard so they hadn't gone to the beach in years except when they went to the Gold Coast on holidays and then Louise spent more time running around after her family than just taking time out for herself. Before she knew what she was doing she had jumped into her car and was driving to the old life saving club. She didn't know why it was calling after all those years but she just knew she had to go there. She had been happy there and if ever she was going to find happiness again it just may be on the beach at Mentone.

The sun was just going down as she pulled into the car park. What a pity, she thought, that I don't live on the west coast or I could be watching the sun setting on the water. Instead she was just standing in front of her car as the daylight faded.

'Tiny, Tiny get back here. Tiny I mean it!'

Without taking much notice she heard the call from the right of her but it was the spray of an overgrown shaggy coat that covered her from head to toe that caught her attention. Suddenly and shockingly.

'Oh my god, are you okay? Tiny I said stop it,' and with that came another fast and furious spray of salty water droplets from the wet coat of one very large, very shaggy, very not so tiny dog. Unbidden from deep within Louise came first a single tear, that slid down her cheek then without knowing what to do came an outpouring of emotion so ferocious that Louise found herself shaking with sobs. The more she tried to stop she found herself gulping for air and the noises which escaped her throat were those of an animal wailing in distress.

Tiny's owner didn't know what to do. He stood silently beside her as even the errant Tiny came to heel at his master's side, lay on the ground and put his head between his paws. After what felt to Louise like ages but was in reality only two minutes the emotion had passed. Her sobs turned to sniffles and finally she had herself in check again. She raised two very red tear stained eyes to a very scared man. Emotional women were not his thing and he wasn't too sure exactly what Tiny had done to initiate such an outburst but he at least knew that to run, as he really wanted to do, would be unwise. His mother had always told him when women were crying it was best to stay silent until he could say or do something constructive. He was not feeling very constructive right now so to him silence was his only option, that and keeping an eye out for her producing any sharp objects.

As Louise looked into his caring and slightly frightened eyes she started to cry again only this time not so loudly. She no longer cared who heard or who saw her. What did it matter now? Everything in her life had changed. Her kids no longer needed her, her husband no longer wanted her and her garden was just fine on its own. She had no job, no life and was nearly forty. She may as well be over the hill. What was left? She was brought up better than this though to just cry into a stranger's face and not even introduce herself. Her mother would have been mortified had she seen her like this.

'I'm sorry. It's not you. It's not even your dog. It's nothing to do with ...' and at this point she burst into another flood of tears.

'Are you hurt, can I call someone?' He noticed she wore a wedding ring so putting one and one together asked, 'Can I call your husband?'

The flash of anguish that came from her eyes told him that probably that was the problem as she resumed sobbing with greater earnest. He hated to see damsels in distress so tentatively he started to pat her shoulder blades. Slowly his pat turned into a small circular motion rub as he had seen his sister do with her children and was surprised at the impact that it had. Louise started to regain whatever composure she had left and raised a tired smile to him.

'You look like you could do with a friendly ear. I'm just over the road. Would you care for a cup of tea or a glass of wine? I promise you I am harmless and you look like someone in need of a friend right now.' With that Louise nodded assent and found herself crossing the road with a complete stranger and the largest dog called Tiny she had ever seen.

Before he opened the door the man turned to Louise.

'Before you come in let me introduce myself. My name is Tom, this is Tiny and this is my house.'

'Thank-you Tom, I'm Louise and I am very embarrassed.'

'Don't be.' After Tom had poured Louise a scotch – she looked as if she could do with a stiff drink – they settled into his lounge room. His house was double storey townhouse with the living areas upstairs overlooking the bay and the bedrooms all downstairs. The views of the bay were magnificent and to add to the ambience of the evening he had an open fire going as well. Louise just knew that she was safe here.

'I have to apologise for Tiny. We had just gone for a run on the beach and he had run into the surf to fetch a stick he thought I had thrown. I was trying to get him home quickly to dry him off and he ran straight up to you. Are you still wet? Do you need to borrow some clothes while yours dry?'

Louise went scarlet. The idea that here she was sitting in a stranger's house was one thing but sitting in her underwear while her clothes dried elsewhere was not something she could imagine herself doing.

'No really I'm fine. I don't know what happened. I used to come to this beach when I was a girl and today I was just feeling kind of you know sad for the old days. And then your dog came up and startled me and the next thing I knew I was howling like a baby. You must have thought that I was mad?'

'To be honest I didn't know what to think. I couldn't work out if it was something the dog did, I did or if you were dying there for a minute.'

'Not you. My husband. He left me about four months ago and I thought I was dealing with it but I guess that I hadn't. My kids left home over a year ago, which is great, then he left home and you know, here I am nearly forty and nothing left to show for my life. I'm virtually over the hill. I need to get a job. But I've never had one. Our business has gone broke so I can't ask him for any money. He is running around with his masseur and I am sitting in this big old house in Balwyn and I was desperate for the sea air again. I was completely lost in thought when your dog bounded up to me and decided to shake some life into or should I say onto me.' Here she gave a giggle for the first time. Tom felt relieved that he could sense her relaxing and there wasn't going to be a reprise of the hysteria that he had witnessed earlier.

'So what are you looking for? What are you good at?'

'I'm no good at anything. I've only ever been a mother and now I'm too old for anything.'

'Too old, that's rubbish. Did anyone tell Mother Theresa she was too old? Age is relative. I bet the pensioners living next door here would love to be your age again. Do you know how many kids are getting knocked back for jobs because they have no experience? You are loaded with experience. If you are a mother and my guess is you are a great Mum then you can organise busy schedules, which makes you great at time management, great at mediating arguments, great at pulling rabbits out of hats when your kids had nothing to do. You were raising your children before computers and Nintendos started to do it instead.'

'Tell me what do you like doing? What is your hobby? Often that is a great place to start.'

'Unbelievable, you sound just like Joy, a friend of mine.'

'Joy sounds like a great woman. So tell me, what is it that excites you?'

'Gardening and painting. I love my garden and I love sitting creating a canvas.'

'Gardening's growing. Why don't you get into gardening?'

'I'm too old for all of that.'

'All of what? Let me guess. You have to be somewhere around your mid thirties. Why do you keep saying you are too old? Keep talking like that and I'll be sending you off to a retirement village.'

'Very funny. I'm 38, see I'm not that old but I couldn't imagine starting a long course and there is no way I can see myself starting a gardening business. What are you suggesting I get a mowing franchise?'

'Wow, you are not thinking outside the square are you?' Tom leant back in his chair and had a sip of his drink. He liked this bedraggled woman but he knew he had to keep it light or she might just as easliy run out into the night and he would never see her again.

'I'm not suggesting a business; mind you, you migt be good at it. More so I was thinking of working in a nursery. You say you love gardening. My guess is you know your local nursery inside and out and can probably even tell them a thing or two about planting in your neighbourhood. Have you considered that?' He looked at this woman, who was relaxing ever so slightly. At the way she tilted her head when she spoke and how she seemed to be so strong and yet so fragile all at the same time.

'Well no I haven't.' Mused Louise finally.

'Then ask them. What have you got to lose and while you are at it have a look at the ages of most of the work force out there. You have not even hit the halfway mark in your work life and already you are thinking you are old. You will grow old quickly if that is how you see yourself. Try looking at your life as a whole. You are not even at your prime yet. You think you are old but remember that you will always be younger than everyone born before you. How do you think they feel when they are getting on with their lives feeling fabulous and you are moaning how old you are? Let go of that wasted thought process.' Tom made Louise feel alive. More alive than she had felt in a long time. The scotches went down a little too well, and the wine with dinner even better.

It was not until the sunlight hit her eyelids the next morning did she realise that there was a chance she had had a little too much wine the night before. She rolled over to fade back into the oblivion of sleep when she realised that all was not as it should be. Memories of the night before started to creep in slowly and when she was confronted with a wet nose against her hand she knew something was completely wrong with this picture. Twice in 14 hours Tiny had shaken her world up. Well actually Tiny had just been the instigator, it was Tom who had shaken her world. Or had he. She was so confused. She was alone in a strange bed which was obviously at his place but he was nowhere to be seen. Had she or hadn't she? She couldn't remember. Oh think Louise, she said to herself. What did happen last night? She heard the front door open and close and a head popped around the corner of the door.

'Good morning. I see you are awake now.' The same warm eyes from last night greeted her as she tried to make sense of exactly how the night had finished.

'Breakfast will be in ten minutes. There is a towel in the bathroom and before you ask, no nothing happened last night. You were in the middle of telling me a lovely story about garden gnomes and your friends from school when you passed out. So once you are finished with your shower you can finish that delightful tale of misadventure.' And with that he went upstairs to the kitchen whistling to himself as he walked.

Chapter 8.

Focus on what's fabulous

Focus on what's fabulous

'Did you hear?' Cynthia said with a wicked gleam in her voice.

'Hear what?' drolly replied Rebecca expecting a flurry of gossip from Cynthia's office.

'Louise has slept with a man.'

'Who, what, how, where, how do you know? I don't believe you.' Rebecca rattled off with the speed and force of a machine gun.

'Sure has, she told me over the weekend. And she said ...' Cynthia broke off at that point as the very woman in question strolled up to them.

'She said nothing of the sort,' said a very fresh faced beaming Louise who was sliding into her seat at the Café Club as Cynthia was looking conspiratorially at Rebecca. Cynthia sat back into her seat. She had been practically in Rebecca's lap as she was spilling the beans on Louise. Both Cynthia and Rebecca angled their bodies squarely on Louise and even Joy slid down from the other end of the bar to listen in and this was a case of obviously listening in. She wasn't even pretending or accidentally hearing the girls on this occasion.

'Well what did you say or should we ask what did you do Miss Louise? Hmm,' asked Rebecca. Where would Louise begin? Tom was like a dream, a fantasy really, something that would happen to one of her friends or in a novel. Not to Louise Smart. Ever since that fateful evening last weekend Louise had seen Tom twice for dinner, again for breakfast and once for lunch. She had not spent another night at his house though. Tom was a builder so he could sneak away from his work sites when he wanted to. He had a large team working for him and hadn't really lifted a tool in the past four years. He was approaching fifty, single and very successful. Luckily for Louise he was only single because his last relationship of ten years had finished only six months earlier. He had no children and surprisingly no emotional baggage. Like Louise he was pretty new to being single as well. He hadn't gone into too many details about his past except to say that after ten years and a hefty settlement they had parted their ways. He did make her laugh and Tiny hadn't frightened her since, though she was still wary of a dog that big. No matter how much Tom said he liked her. That dog could double as a pony.

'Well did you or didn't you? You said you stayed the night, what gives?,' pushed Cynthia.

'I didn't sleep with him. I passed out drunk on him and he put me to bed in the spare room at his place. It was all very nice.'

'Nice, shmice. You should have shagged him senseless. Gotten that ex out of your system for good. That's what I would've done. You know nice is a four letter word in my books and you remember what Sister James would say to us about using four letter words at school.'

'Cynthia he is just a friend. I'm moving slowly. I'm not like you. I've never bed hopped. There was only ever Rob and you know the trouble I got into sleeping with him. I can't risk that again. Oh my, condoms, the pill, this is a whole world I know nothing about. I got Rob snipped 10 years back so we had no extra surprises to worry about.' When it was put like that the girls realised that Louise was entering a foreign land so they thought they should lay off for a while. She'd find her own way and if she didn't, she would ask them. Or so they hoped. For isn't that what girlfriends were for; advice on recipes, broken hearts and contraception? At least that was how it used to be.

Joy came to their table with their coffees. They all had standing orders so it was easy to get started. She had one of her casuals come in early on a Thursday to allow her a chance to sit with the girls. Interruptions were annoying and it was not as if she couldn't afford to take some time at this time of day.

'Well ladies I think we know what Louise has been up to over the past fortnight. Rebecca, you've been pretty quiet. How have you been and what is happening in your world?'

Rebecca gave all of the girls a beaming smile, pushed her hair off her shoulders and straightened up. 'You won't believe the couple of weeks I've had. As you know it's been school holidays and I thought it would be a nightmare but surprisingly it wasn't. I took your advice on my body shape and bought myself a few new tops that were more fitted, grabbed a couple of those new long lasting lip glosses and a couple of new pairs of pants. Some jeans and sort of winter cargos. I've stopped wearing those shapeless t-shirts and I've been getting comments that everyone thinks I have lost weight. I'll admit I have lost about three kilos since we began which is not a huge amount but everything was starting to get not just comfortable again but a little bit loose. I even had some tradies down the road from my place whistle at me as I went to pick the boys up.'

'Careful Bec that may have been Lou's man you were attracting. What sort of tradies were they anyway? I don't mind a man with muscles.'

'Cyn, you don't mind a man with a heartbeat. Settle down anyway Tom isn't working anywhere near Rebecca's. Go on Becs.' Louise liked the way Tom's name sprung from her lips. It had a nice ring to it.

'As I was saying,' continued Rebecca, 'So I've got the tradies whistling, my boys are wondering if we are going somewhere special because I am all dolled up and Justin practically dragging me down the hallway to our room each night all because of a little bit of lipstick and clothes that fit.'

'Bravo,' said Joy, 'This is what I was hoping for. Noticeable differences in your lives just through a few small changes. Has this been hard so far?'

'No,' the girls echoed. Louise included a small giggle. She was enjoying herself more and relaxing more now than she had in ages.

Joy continued, 'You all could have done this all along on your own. It's not magic.'

'I don't know about that. It was definatley some kind of magic that introduced me to Tom,' said Louise. 'How would I have ever had the guts to meet a man like him if you hadn't started getting us looking and thinking more about ourselves.'

'Louise, thanks for the credit but I think you forget it was your love of the sea and his great shaggy dog that I believe did all of the introductions.' Joy moved her attention from Louise to Cynthia. 'So Cynthia, your past couple of weeks, were you going through the same changes the other two experienced?'

'So so,' stated Cynthia. 'Nothing as exciting as these two I am afraid. I had a cold so I stayed in last weekend and while I thought there was a chance I was going to get my own clients nothing has come of it. Oh, before I forget can we make it an hour later next time? I've got a meeting to attend first so I have to go in that morning?'

'Louise, Rebecca do you mind if we move the time for Cynthia?' The girls were both in agreement so the focus turned back to Cynthia and her musings over the past couple of weeks.

'I must say though I feel as if I am at a finishing school or something. That stuff we talked about last time. You know about our body shapes and the glasses has me now looking at the other girls in the office and how their clothes sometimes suit them and sometimes don't. Tell me is it because men are made up of straight lines that the suit suits them so well and not as well as us girls. Unless you have flat chest a boxy jacket can really make a girl look very dumpy without the right tailoring.'

'That's right.' Joy smiled at how quickly the girls were picking up on her advice. 'In fact you have opened us up to the point of today's session very nicely thanks Cynthia. Today we are going to focus on exactly what we focus on and how you find that by your choice in clothing you can take the eye to or away from wherever you like.' The girls all looked excitedly at each other and then turned three sets of eager eyes to Joy for more information.

'Did you girls all realise that you are all roughly the same size?' The girls all shook their heads; they did not understand what Joy was saying. As far as they could tell they all had different bodies. In fact wasn't that the object of their last session? Not one of them was the same shape.

It was Rebecca who broke the silence. 'Joy, if I understand you correctly you are saying that we are different shapes but the same size. I don't get it?'

'Okay let's begin. If the three of you stood up you would be roughly the same height. Correct?' The girls looked at each other. It was obvious to them sitting there that Rebecca was taller, and then came Louise while Cynthia appeared to be the shortest at the table.

'Can the three of you stand up please and face the mirror along the wall behind you.' Obediently, if not a little embarrassed, the three girls stood up and were amazed to see that they were all exactly the same height.

'How does that work? When we were sitting Rebecca appeared to be so much taller,' Cynthia asked as she hated to think of herself as short.

'The truth is that your bodies are built differently. Cynthia you have longer legs which will make your torso shorter than Rebecca who has shorter legs and a longer torso and then there is Louise in the middle who is balanced between her torso and her legs. This will immediately mean that each of you will wear the same clothes differently and will look different. Cynthia if you wear a short cropped jacket you will appear to be taller as so much more of your legs will be visible. Add a pair of heels and you could start to look like an ostrich. All top heavy, especially with your pronounced shoulders. You will look more balanced in a longer jacket. Rebecca, while you probably prefer to wear a longer jacket so that you can hide your bottom you would find a jacket that came to mid thigh will make you appear shorter as you have less thigh and calf as the other two girls. Louise you can go shorter or longer depending on how you feel on the day. Rebecca you would look slimmer and taller if your jackets came to your hip rather than your thighs. Each of you will need different necklines as well. Louise and Cynthia, the fact that you have smaller busts mean a higher neckline will give you the appearance of a fuller bust than say if Rebecca was to wear a high neckline. With her full bust she will appear to have a shelf forming above her ribcage. She will suit lower necklines to lessen the impact of her bust.' Louise who had never considered herself a fashionista was getting into the mood of these sessions and responded to the information she heard quickly.

'So that will explain why when I wore scooped and low tops I looked like a 12 year old. My breasts were never very large, except when I was breastfeeding but since the kids they seem to have flattened out even further. I thought it was the breast feeding. Are you saying that I have looked so flat all of these years because of my tops?'

'Well yes and no. Breastfeeding will do various things to a woman. Some will result in larger breasts.' At this Rebecca raised her hand and nodded in agreement, 'some women will get smaller flatter breasts and some will go back to exactly the same shape as before.'

'Louise, come with me, I'm going to help you find the best bra to make you appear larger and fuller. Check me out. No one would know I was only a B cup.' Cynthia proudly threw her shoulders back, straightened her back, lifted her chin and displayed her bust for all to admire. It was true Cynthia appeared to have a fuller bust than Louise and the trick was just in her bra and neckline.

'Oh, I don't know that I could go that far.' Cynthia's posture was a bit more than Louise was comfortable with. 'But I wouldn't mind getting some shape. I'm tired of looking like I have nothing.'

'And now that you have Tommy you want him to admire your boobies. Don't pretend.' Only Cynthia could get away with a comment like that as Louise went bright red and hunched her shoulders even further forward.

'You can create focus even with your sleeve length. Take for example a short sleeve. If it stops at your bust line it will create a horizontal line across your bust bringing your bust even more into focus. Just like if you had pockets over your boobs or carried a handbag under your arm. Anything that creates a focal point or a horizontal line across your body should be used if you want to bring the attention there or avoided if you do not. I like to think of every part of your body as an asset. Some of you will have assets you want the world to see and some parts of you, you will want to keep hidden. These are your hidden assets. Accountants know all about hidden assets.'

Louise joined in at this point. 'I'm hoping my accountant can find Rob's hidden assets. Did you know he has moved into a rental at the Docklands? How can he afford that when we apparently have nothing left? I had only ever thought of hidden assets as hidden money.'

'Your hidden assets are those parts of you that only you know you have and no one else is aware of. Just like what it appears Rob may have hiding as well. Let's hope your accountant can find what Rob is hiding. But let's worry only about how you look for today. Ladies do you mind sharing with me the parts of yourself which I am sure you will think everyone is noticing but I am sure you will be surprised how little we do. Whatever they are though we'll discuss how you can manage to conceal these parts of you that you would like to keep hidden from the rest of the world. What I want you to do is stand up and tell us what you don't like and would like to hide. Who wants to go first?' Never one to sit back quietly, Cynthia jumped up and stood in front of the girls.

'Okay. What I hate about myself ...'

'Before we go any further, I don't want you hating any part of yourself. You are all perfect. I want you to love every part of yourself.

That is why we are talking about hidden assets. These are not liabilities. You must be proud of the body you have because unless you spend money with a plastic surgeon this is the only body you will ever have so you have to be proud of it, respect it and love every part of it. You just don't have to expose every part of it.' Cynthia acknowledged what Joy had said and started again.

'All right what I love about myself but you don't have to know about are how really small my boobs are. Can you see how short my neck is and I would love a teeny tiny waist not this trunk that passes through my middle.' She stood with her hands on her waist to illustrate how it did not dip in at all.

'Thank you Cynthia. What you have pointed out to us we have never noticed but as they are parts of yourself that you would like to camouflage let's get down to it. I think we have covered some of how you can improve your breasts. You are spot on with finding great brassieres, they can make the smallest breasts appear fuller. A higher neckline or in your case a more revealing neckline will also do the trick. However this is not appropriate when you are at work. Steer clear of high collared shirts as they will make your neck appear shorter and avoid wearing a choker necklace to make your neck appear longer. As you have longer legs and a small bust you'll find longer necklaces will bring attention to your bust and take the focus from your neck. When it comes to creating a defined waist, that is most effectively done by wearing a belt around your middle. You could also wear different blocks of colour top and bottom thereby creating a break at your middle and drawing the eye there. Finally you can create a waist by finding clothing that has seams that come in closer at your waist and appear to narrow the garment at that point. Three quarter sleeve tops will bring the eye to your waist and in your case I would avoid them as you want to keep the eyes further up so I would chose short or long sleeves if I was you.' Cynthia smiled. She liked those options and the thought of getting more jewellery to hang around her neck sounded fun.

'Louise, Rebecca, who wants the next spot?' Rebecca desperately wanted to rediscover her old shape and if today's session could bring her a step closer to achieving this goal she wasn't going to wait a second longer. 'I'm in,' she piped up and took Cynthia's place standing in front of everyone.

'So Rebecca, what is it that you would like to keep under wraps about your body. What are to be your hidden assets?'

'As if you can't tell. Boobs, belly and bum.' Her hands followed her words to each part of her body then dropped to her side as she finished. She felt she had revealed herself to the world in those three words. She inclined her head to the right and took everyone's faces in as they assessed her figure. It was true Rebecca had some weight on her bottom and her stomach was not as flat as it had been but Cynthia and Louise were shocked to hear her mention her breasts. What they wouldn't have given to even have half of what Rebecca had. Unable to hold herself back Cynthia had to ask why Rebecca wanted to conceal her magnificent bosom. If they were hers she would have had them out for the world to admire.

'Cyn, you try growing up with these girls. Ever since I was thirteen people have noticed my bust before my face. The amount of men who spoke to me at chest level especially when I was in my twenties was a joke. Yes it is nice to have them but I don't want to hang them out for the world to see.'

'Fair enough but just for a day it would be fun. Imagine what I could get up to when I went out!' Cynthia quipped.

'Cynthia you are unbelievable. Leave them alone alright,' Rebecca said.

'Okay, but I don't get it.' Cynthia responded, 'If you've got it flaunt it.'

'Cynthia!' Rebecca could not beleive her friend could still be going on about breasts at her age.

'All right, okay I get it, you don't want the girls out.' Cynthia, always one for the last word ended.

'Joy can you slap her for me,' asked Rebecca good naturedly. Joy raised her hand and in a mock slap. Cynthia finally settled down again. One day she would settle down thought Joy to herself. It would be a pity to tame her but for her to get ahead in her career it would be necessary. But that will be another session Joy decided.

'Rebecca, I heard what you asked about and it is all very do-able.' A smile formed at Rebecca's mouth. She didn't hate her figure, but she would prefer to return to the silhouette she used to have and until that time she would settle for the illusion of that shape.

'Let's start in the order you gave. Again I think we have discussed yours and everyone else's breasts in detail up 'til now, thanks to Cynthia. I would like to add if you want to achieve an even smaller bust do as Cynthia did and get a great fitting brassiere. The right one has the power to not only give you more shape, it can reduce your shape and it can make you appear instantly slimmer once you have your bust sitting away from your body. The amount of women who buy a bra and never again adjust their straps is beyond me. When they buy it they look fabulous and then they wonder what has happened as their shape starts to sag. It is important to adjust your straps every time you put your bra on and to put yourself into it properly when you are fitted. Doing the back up in the front and pushing your hooks around to the back then sliding your arms into the straps is not the right way. Lean down into your bra before you take the straps around to your back and you will have a great shape. Now to your belly. You need to adopt the opposite of what Cynthia has to do. Avoid wearing a different colour top and bottom as this will bring the focus to your belly and waist area. You want colour to go straight through that area. Make sure your clothing is not too tight there. If you can move your clothes easily around your middle you will be creating an illusion of a finer figure. Avoid anything that is tight at your waist. For the time being when you are wearing tops and bottoms leave your tops out. Don't tuck them in, otherwise you may end up with the hint of a muffin top and that is not a good look.'

The girls all looked at Joy with raised eyebrows. 'Muffin top,' said Cynthia, 'I thought you would have something far more elegant to use to describe the rolls of fat that hang over our waist bands.'

'Why should I? I know what a muffin top means and it is very descriptive.' The girls all had to agree with that logic as Joy continued. 'So, as I was saying, keep the colours similar or the same over that area. Lastly, to make your bottom appear smaller it is the same theory. You don't want to create any horizontal lines across your bottom. Avoid jackets that finish at the fullest part of your buttocks. Minimal pleating and gathering in your skirts. Keep the focus up high with great earrings and necklaces until you feel you are happy to display your bottom again. To be honest, it is not that bad but it is all perception as to how you feel about it.'

'When you said that Joy, you reminded me of the mad mirrors that I was looking in at Luna Park last week with the boys. You know the ones that you stand in front of and one minute you are tall and skinny and the next you are short and fat. I hate those mirrors, mind you I wouldn't mind having a tall and skinny mirror in my bedroom for when I get dressed in the morning. It would instantaneously lift my mood for the day.'

'Perceptions are nine tenths, if not more, of the problems that we have today. Ever since we are born we are bombarded with images of how we should and shouldn't look. Every magazine will give you a different slant on what is in or out and what you must have for the season. The problem is unless you have the exact figure of the models on the covers of those magazines you are never going to look like them and instead of saying I am me, most women think, I am wrong. I failed. What's wrong with me? Did you realise women made their own clothes until around the First World War. After that they started mass production of clothing and it is only since mass production came in did women become more fixated on their shape than ever before. You see before that everything article of clothing they had was made by them or for them and so it fitted perfectly. Once you get into mass production it is too hard to fit every figure so they create general fit and make you feel inferior if you do not fit their shape. That is why I tell you that everything about you is beautiful and perfect for you.'

'That may be so but it is no perception of mine that my bottom has gotten bigger over the past seven years. My pants, which no longer fit me testify to that fact. This is no illusion, this is reality.' Rebecca ended sadly.

'Rebecca do you think you look that terrible?' Joy asked kindly.

'Not really. Look, I know there are women out there who are bigger than me but the fact is that I am currently bigger than the me I feel inside. The me I am used to and the me I want to become again. Is that so wrong?'

Joy could hear her concern and quickly brought her attention back to what she could do. 'No not wrong at all. I just want you to stop focusing on what's not working and start focusing on what is. Can you do that for me pet.'

'I can do that. And anyway if I can't get the pants I like I can still buy the shoes I love.' Rebecca was a glass half full kind of girl so she never stayed down for long. It was now Louise's turn to expose her physical shortcomings to her friends. She was not as self conscious as the other two so she stood comfortable in front of them in her cream linen slacks and rust coloured woollen jumper with her mocha brown suede boots on. She stood with her hands on her hips and announced clearly. 'Come on Joy. Make me gorgeous.'

'No problem, Before I get to that tell me Louise what do you wish to remain a secret from society.'

'That's easy, my chunky cankles and my fat upper arms.'

'Your cankles? And what pray tell are you cankles dear?' asked Joy.

'My ankles which are as full as my calves. I have no definition there.'

'Consider it done!' With that Joy made a flourish as if wielding a magic wand at Louise as she stood in front of the women. 'I wish it was that easy but let me give you the tips that are ideal for your needs. I like to start at the top and work my way down so we'll start with your arms. You obviously have these two areas of your body under control because I had no idea of either.'

'I do. I wear long sleeves and try to wear long pants all of the time. That is another reason why I hate to wear skirts. Aside from which as I now know I am a relaxed personality they clashed with the inner Louise.' Louise was having so much fun today. It was obvious to all that Tom was having a very positive influence on their friend.

'So tell me do you want to wear skirts at all and would you like to wear shorter sleeves?' Joy asked, for if the answers were no to both her work was done for the day.

'I might like to wear a dress once in a while and over summer I might want to wear something lighter if I am being taken out for dinner.'

'Careful Louise, it sounds as if your internal Feminine may be peeking through.' Louise gave a mock shock horror expression which got all of them laughing. Joy loved how the girls were taking the information in so comfortably. 'It's okay Louise we actually have a percentage of all of the personalities within all of us. It is just dependent on how much and when they come out. It isn't unusual to have a degree of Femininity emerge especially when you are dating. It is a primal thing. Don't worry you won't go all frilly on us overnight or even over time. Your primary personality is fixed.'

'Thank goodness for that or I had my hair all cut off for nothing.'

'But now to the task at hand – how to work with those assets of yours, your arms. Ideally covering your upper arm will always be the easiest. However if you want to wear a shorter sleeve, try a sleeve which comes to just above your elbow but below the fullest part of your bicep. Avoid any sleeves stopping at that point of your arm or even an empire line clothing as the line under the bust can create a horizontal line drawing attention to your arms. A fuller bell shaped short sleeve will make your arms appear smaller and finally if you are going out to an evening function a very sheer wrap worn twisted around your upper arms can be a great concealer. Your ankles are also an easy fix. Again trousers are an option but here it is more about what to avoid that what to do. When you chose heels look for a shoe with a thicker heel as a fine heel will only accentuate the size of your ankle. You will find that you suit a shoe with more substance to it than a delicate shoe. During cooler weather you can wear long boots with your skirts or dark tights under skirts are another option. Your personality is such that you will wear more trousers than not so just keep those few points in mind and if you have trouble knowing where to find any of the shoes I mentioned just ask Rebecca or Cynthia, I'm pretty sure they will know where to find what you are looking for. Remember girls, when you are wearing shoes with a coloured outfit then you should wear shoes the same colour as the outfit or your hair colour to complete the outfit. Rebecca with your dark hair you will always look better in a darker shoe than a lighter shoe and Cynthia you'll look great in a pair of shoes that are camel or a blonde tone when you have colours on if you cannot match the outfit. It's a top and tailing sort of look.'

The girls were amazed at the tid bits of information Joy shared with them. They never knew what was coming next.

It was late in the afternoon now and Rebecca had to go to be home when her boys came in. They hastily said their goodbyes and each went their separate ways after they left the café. Joy was left with the memory of the afternoon and the hope that what she was doing was benefiting the girls as much as it was benefiting her. It had been a long time since she had felt so alive. Not since her William was alive, and it felt good.

Chapter 9.

More than groceries

More than groceries

Rebecca was in the kitchen when her boys raced in the door. The witching hours had begun. Bedlam would now take over in her household until around 8pm by which time she knew that both boys were safely tucked up in bed. It was then that she wanted to talk to Justin about her life. While she missed her old life she knew she couldn't go back to flying. The hours were too irregular and she liked being home with her boys. The idea of an overnight in Darwin sounded luscious especially as it was still winter here in Melbourne and she hated the cold but the thought of leaving home before her boys were up and not arriving home until after they were in bed the next day was too much. Her life had certainly changed. She remembered back to when the boys were solely reliant on her how she had dreamt of finally getting some time to herself. Only now that it was here she hardly knew what to do with herself. Her days seemed dull. She didn't have to go to work and she didn't have to do multiple loads of washing every day. And there was only so much housework she could do before she was cleaning clean spaces again. She was, however, enjoying taking care of herself. It had reignited something within her. This wasn't vanity but a part of her she had put to sleep while she was so engrossed with the raising of her babies. They were no longer babies and it was time for her to awaken that part of her that got excited by life. She was so afraid if she ever said this to anyone that they would think she was a bad mother. She loved her boys more than anything and would do anything for them and if it meant putting her wants and needs aside for the rest of her life she would have done so without a second thought. The truth though was now they didn't require her every second of the day so that little part of Rebecca that was her identity was awakening. She could feel a slight stirring within of the desire to do something and be someone again. But exactly what she had no idea.

The boys raced past her, flinging their school bags into the hall and racing into their bedrooms. In a flash they were running around the house yelling at each other. This game had started recently and Rebecca had thought it was fun at first. They had played in a similar vein when they were babies but the yells were not so loud and the way they played physically with each other had not seemed as rough. Her boys always had a snack when they got home. This afternoon Rebecca had Vegemite sandwiches and a glass of apple juice for them. She stepped in front to get their attention only to find that they paid her scant notice and kept playing. Rebecca raised her voice but to no avail. Now that she thought about it this was not new behaviour, it had been escalating for some time. Only last week, both boys had to be asked numerous times to put down their Nintendo DS's and come to the table. Then the week before she had had to turn the television off to get their attention. When had all this started she thought to herself? Was she in denial that her angels had become devils? She had never spoken to anyone about the boys behaving like this as she thought it was just standard behaviour for young boys. But at what age does it stop being games and the inattention of youth and when does it turn to downright disobedience? After she had yelled at them for what felt like half an hour but was in reality only about five minutes, the two boys stopped and looked at her as if they were seeing her for the first time. She motioned to them to have their snacks which they inhaled and then they ran into the play room to engage in battle with each other on their Playstation.

Justin came in at his usual hour. They spent the evening as they always did as a family firstly by sharing their meal at the kitchen table and then making sure the boys did their homework. In Jacob's case she would help him practise his reading and Justin would test his spelling before he went to bed. Luke was enjoying his classes and his teacher said he was easily distracted but overall a good student. They had nothing to worry about at this age. The boys were being boys. If they came home exhausted they would go to bed easily but if they spent the afternoon on their computer games often they weren't tired and it would drive Rebecca to distraction trying to get them to bed. School holidays were the worst and thankfully they were now over and she could relax somewhat again.

The football season was coming to a close. It was hard enough running around after the boys at home. Her life as a personal chauffer, butler and maid to the boys was taking its toll. Jacob was playing Auskick every weekend so she had him at the field by 9am. Luke was playing in the under 10s on either a Saturday or Sunday. It was often best if he played at the same time so that Justin could take one and she the other and then it was done for the weekend. They had the rest of the weekend for themselves. Mind you more and more the boys were spending time with friends so she was forever shuffling them between friends and sporting activities. Soon it would be time to pull out their cricket whites for summer. They were growing up so quickly. Only the other day during their school holidays Luke had asked if he could go to the movies with his friends. That was not on but she at least allowed them to sit in the cinema on their own and she went shopping while she waited. She remembered when she was a girl she used to go to Southland with her friends as well. Only back then it was one fifth of its current size if not smaller than it was now. She remembered that it had a roof top garden you could go to on the sunny days and was only located on one side of the Nepean Highway. Many Saturdays were spent hanging out at the shops there mainly because the shops closed at 1pm on a Saturday and there was no Sunday trading in those days. Raising her boys was becoming more and more challenging. With the new school term Luke had started exerting his boyhood, because she certainly couldn't call him a man yet but he was trying to act like one. Funny how he had sounded so like his father when he explained that he no longer needed her to take him to school, he could walk on his own. Luckily they were down the road from the school so Rebecca relented and allowed the two boys to walk straight to school while she waited at the front gate and watched them. She had also taken to standing at the front gate to watch them come home. Before she knew it they would not even need that sort of guidance but that would not be until they were both a few years older. It was interesting to see their expressions when it was raining the other morning and she told them that she wouldn't be driving them to school in the rain. Of course she had no intention of doing that but for a minute she let them think she did. A glimmer of fear at having to face the elements crossed their faces and the relief they felt when she admitted that she had no intention of letting them walk in the rain was clear to see. She was wondering if she had let them off the hook too soon. Was she playing them or were they playing her? Luke you could read like a book but it was Jacob who she was never too sure about. Even when he was in kindergarten his teacher had said of all the children she had ever cared for he was one that she had to take his word for how he felt. His teacher could never tell if he was play acting or serious. He was a charmer and a born actor. She would have to keep an eye on him or he was going to start getting his own way too often without her even realising what he was doing. As they grew up she expected Jacob to be more trouble than Luke. Luke was a simple boy, like his Dad. Black and white and very loving. There was no subterfuge or scheming where he was concerned.

Once the boys were in bed, Justin and Rebecca settled onto the couch to watch their favourite shows. Rebecca couldn't lose herself in the mindlessness of evening television as tonight she had things on her mind. She wanted to talk to Justin about the boys and about getting a job. When it came to the boys Justin could not understand what she was worrying about. He was sure he was the same at their age and that they were just being boys. His answer was to tell him when and if they were uncontrollable again and he would handle it. Rebecca knew that he was trying to help but felt that his solution was not an answer only a band-aid approach.

She loved Justin just as he loved her but was he really seeing her as the woman she was now or the girl he had met in her mid twenties. The girl who filled her days working, shopping and having lunch with her girlfriends. Working for an airline did have its perks. She remembered fondly a Perth overnight. She was crewing the flight with one of her best friends and the another couple of friends didn't want to miss out so they came over as passengers just so the four of them could have lunch together. This led to the four of them having lunch and partying in Perth. She still had a photo of the girls and the whole crew taken in the lobby of the hotel somewhere in one of her photo albums. She should pull it out and scan it into her digital photo frame.

The girls still caught up for special occasions just as she had with Cynthia and Louise once they left school. Her friendship with her flying friends though started to fade in regularity after she left the airline. She could not say the friendships were gone but as with anything when there is a change in lifestyle, your life has to accommodate new needs, new challenges and new people. Her single lifestyle was pertinent for the time she was flying but no longer relevant to the mother of two rambunctious boys. She had accepted this fact years ago. It was not that life she wanted back but she did want something for herself. She hadn't realised how little aside from the boys there really was in her life. Justin, bless him, wanted to help but he did not see what the problem was. His solution was to call the girls and plan lunch. Rebecca knew she needed more but was not exactly sure what that was.

The next morning Rebecca was to find her answer in the most unexpected way. It was Friday and it was her day to do her shopping for the week. It was likely due to the fact that from an early age both boys had had crèche on a Friday for a full day and she had got into the habit of shopping when she was free from the boys. It also allowed her to fill the pantry with fresh food for the weekend and leave that time free to spend with all of her boys, Justin included.

Rebecca loved doing her grocery shopping. Cooking was her passion and just being in the supermarket was a cathartic experience for her. As long as she was alone. Bringing the boys with her, well, root canal was preferable in many ways. When she was alone she would wander along each aisle with her list in hand, looking at what specials were available and conjuring up fabulous meals in her head for their next dinner party. She had popped out of the breads and health foods aisle and was heading into the fresh food section when she saw a tasting booth for a new salami. She loved these tasting booths. Rebecca had started buying many new products simply from enjoying an in-store tasting. She stopped pushing her trolley and stood beside the display savouring the flavours she was being offered. Rebecca stood there and patiently listened to the spiel on the product from the woman with the plastic gloves on her fingers and peaked cap on her head. Rebecca was about to push her trolley away to continue her shopping when on impulse she engaged the woman in conversation about more than her salami. Rebecca discovered that an in-store demonstrator was a casual job that required no previous experience. It did not require you to be 18 and a size 6 and best of all most tastings occurred during school hours so she could be home in time for the boys when they finished school. It sounded ideal. She loved meeting people, she was well trained in customer service and knew how to handle food. Rebecca had found the answer to her question. She could start making her own money again and start living for herself without having to give up any part of her life that was precious to her. She finished her shopping quickly so that she could get home and do some more research into becoming an in-store demonstrator. This was perfect. She couldn't wait to tell Joy and the girls, oh and Justin too.

While Rebecca was thrilled to have made progress in her career development goals Cynthia was experiencing developments of her own. That same Friday morning Cynthia went into the office as usual only to see Mike sitting in reception. If Cynthia hadn't stopped to get a coffee from the coffee kiosk in the foyer she would have been unexpectedly early. The queue of people had held her up and the clock was just hitting 8.30am as she walked through the electronic doors of reception. Lyn was in a meeting this morning so it wasn't really important her being exactly on time. Anyway she was in the building at 8.30am so technically she was there, just not at her desk. Seeing Mike brought a smile to her face. Whether he had a girlfriend or a wife didn't detract from the fact that Cynthia thought that he was incredibly handsome and a great guy. There was no harm in casual flirting until he made it clear if he was single or not.

'Well good morning Mr, oh that's right I never got your surname the other night you raced off into the evening like Cinderella at midnight.'

'Why Madam, how rude of me. To think we spoke without a formal introduction. How remiss of me and how shall I distinguish myself in your good graces if you do not allow me the opportunity to re-address this oversight on my behalf. Let me introduce myself to you. My name is Mr Michael Cere but you may call me Mike.' With that he bowed, took her hand and lightly touched his lips to it. Cynthia didn't know whether to be impressed or appalled. Was he an absolute nutter or a genuine guy with a great sense of humour? The glint in his eyes and the wide grin that spread across his face as he came up from her hand clearly let her see that his sense of humour was alive and well.

Together they laughed and to complete the introduction she dropped a short curtsey and said, 'Why Sir, I accept your gracious introduction. In the absence of a guardian to handle these matters may

I introduce myself to you? My name is Cynthia Fulham and my friends call me Cynful, but you may call me whenever you like.'

It appeared that Mike was in the foyer with the sole purpose of running into her again as he had finalised the discussions he had been having in her office. He was hoping they could have lunch together one day the following week. Cynthia was ready to accept and said she could fit him in this week but he was not available. He would be busy all week and away that coming weekend. With this in mind they made a lunch date for the next Wednesday. Wow, thought Cynthia, will I have something to tell the girls next week. Smiling back at Mike she walked down the hall to her desk, not even noticing that it was now 8.45am and she was certainly late to start her day. She also noticed that she had never had a first date over lunch. This was something new.

Chapter 10。

I can't hear you

I can't hear you

The freshness of spring was in the air and the blossom on the trees in Louise's garden was just about to explode into a cascade of pink and white. Louise loved this time of year. You could almost smell spring. The hint of fine weather in the crisp chill of the morning replaced the overwhelming heaviness of rain and winter's wind. Louise's back wall was covered in a climbing pink rose which, by the middle of summer, was ablaze of colour. The plum trees in her back garden were just starting to fill with blossom. It felt as if overnight her garden became a wonderland of colour. One time as the blossom was finishing a high wind came through and in a single afternoon she witnessed the blossom swirling around her garden like a snow storm. The memory still brought a smile to her face.

Thank goodness it was Thursday. Tom had asked her a question last weekend and she didn't know what to say. Louise was relying on the girls and Joy to help her decide what to do.

She walked from her car to the café thinking about last night and the lovely dinner they had sitting in the warmth of the lounge at Tom's overlooking the bay. Tom was quite the cook; he had prepared Atlantic salmon with a crispy seared skin, a puree of potato and pumpkin with flat beans and poured a Sauvignon Blanc from the Marlborough region of New Zealand. He served pears poached in red wine for dessert with thick lashings of King Island double cream. They finished their meal with coffee and whisper thin after dinner mints. She still hadn't slept with him and Tom seemed to be in no hurry. She had never slept with anyone except Rob and was frankly nervous about how to. It wasn't the act she was nervous about. She couldn't imagine that it would be the same and to be honest she really hoped it wasn't but how do you begin something like that. She might talk to Cynthia about it. She didn't seem to have any problems.

The café had a table of men at the far end as Louise walked in. Joy was serving them coffees and they appeared to be deep in conversation about something. Louise smiled to herself that Joy's was becoming more than just a coffee house. It was the place to go to find the answers to Life. Maybe Joy was the answer to the meaning of Life. The men kept talking as Louise walked by. Not that she hoped for anything but a casual glance might have been nice. Her hair was starting to grow a bit. She would have to get it chopped again and maybe a bit shorter this time. Louise was wearing a new red trench coat, taupe trousers, red boots and a cream jumper. She was having more fun than she had had in a long while. If only she could find a job. She had applied to loads of small nurseries around her but no one had any vacancies. In fact many were closing as the drought was affecting their sales. Now she knew what Joy was trying to tell her when she said that she would find her dream job in her passion. It was Tom who pointed out to her that if she liked gardening so much then she should do it as a job. Why hadn't she started sooner?

She was early so she slid into her seat and waited for Joy to finish. She had time to think about Tom's question. Even if it did make her feel uncomfortable.

Louise waved at Rebecca who was passing the window on her way in. In the short time they had been catching up it was obvious Rebecca had lost some weight. She had on her yoga pants, a lilac windcheater, her hair held back with an Alice band and her trademark lipstick. She never went anywhere now without her lipstick.

Out of breath, Rebecca smiled and waved to Joy as she slumped into her seat.

'Finally the boys are back at school so I can get some things done. I am so busy this week. What with running around after the boys with sports, doing pizzas on Tuesdays, pavlovas yesterday and I have pizzas again tomorrow.'

'I'm sorry, pizzas, pavlovas? What are you talking about?' Without meaning to Louise had barked at Rebecca. She couldn't help herself after raising two kids and a loser for a husband there were times when she forgot the niceties and could be considered abrupt. Rebecca knew her friend and totally ignored her tome. Must be that time of the month or something she thought to herself.

'Oh, I forgot to tell you. I have a job!' With that she smiled one of her award winning smiles which no doubt went a long way for her as a food demonstrator.

'Job, what job? You've got a job! That's great.' At this Cynthia walked in to the café. The table of engrossed men all watched as one as Cynthia, in her knee high black patent boots, fishnet stockings, grey wool mini skirt, grey marle long sleeve tee and her plum coloured cropped jacket took her seat. Neither Louise nor Rebecca missed the impact Cynthia had on her admiring public and shared a glance at each other acknowledging this fact.

'Cyn, how do you do it?' quizzed Louise. 'Becs and I barely rated a glance and you virtually gave each one of those men whiplash as you walked through.'

'What? Who? Oh them, did they? I never even noticed.' That was not exactly true. Cynthia knew the impact she had on men and she used it to her advantage. She didn't, however, notice every reaction especially if her mind was elsewhere and this was one of those occasions. 'Ladies look at yourselves, you both look nice and we are not going back to that four letter word again are we, Lou? I must say you look smashing but not in a sexy kind of head turning way and Becs what's with the gym clothes. I thought you were dressing up these days?'

'Give me a break. I had to get my exercise in some time. Anyway, what are you doing here so early. You said you were going to be late. Was your meeting cancelled?' Rebecca knew her news could wait. Cynthia obviously had something on her mind.

'We finished early. Thankfully.' answered Cynthia with a smile.

'You mean to say you went to work like that?' Rebecca had to get a dig in especially after the comment about her not looking special.

'Like what? This? What's wrong with it? I'll admit it is 90% what I wore out last night but I couldn't help it. I haven't been home yet.'

'Dare we ask what the missing 10% is?' asked Joy who had now taken residence at her end of the bar again.

'I popped into Target and grabbed some fresh knickers and stockings. You can't go commando in a skirt like this. I'm not that stupid and I draw the line at wearing my knickers two days in a row.' Cynthia, for all her femininity could sometimes be very crass. And making a reference to wearing no knickers did manage to get the heads bobbing up from the other table of men. The absurdity of that last comment amused all the women present. While Cynthia would draw the line at recycling her underwear she didn't mind going to work in the clothes she went out in the night before. 'So as I was saying we went to this fab new bar in South Yarra, then on to Eve in South Melbourne. It was Wednesday night yet it was packed. There must have been something on around town. Faces I hadn't seen in years were out. Or else it is the end of winter. Are you feeling it? I am. It feels like summer is just around the corner. Not surprising what with Christmas decorations starting to come onto the shelves. Just this morning I saw them starting to bring into the shops all the decorations. It amazes me how long we get bombarded with all of this media, consumerism hype. What happened to a quiet Christmas singing carols and having dinner with the family? Nowadays my calendar is booked from mid November until after the New Year by October. I tell you there must be something in the air, why only last week I heard that Paul in accounts is seeing Susy in administration. Susy was going out with David from the legal firm on the tenth floor but it appears she caught him having lunch with Lucy from the shoe shop on the corner. I told her she couldn't trust him. You can never trust anyone with a pointy nose. They probe into everything. So, anyway as I was telling Loren last night ...'

Joy threw her hands into the air. 'Cynthia stop. What is with you today? The clothes, the gabbling, the everything?' Cynthia furrowed her forehead. As she saw it everything was fine. There were no problems but for Joy to stop her in that manner she wondered what she may have done. She looked at the other two girls and they just stared back at her.

'Have I done something wrong? Because if I have done something wrong you have to tell me?' Cynthia, sat back into her seat, like a child awaiting a lecture from her teacher.

'Messages. There are mixed messages all around this table today so I think we need to focus on what you are saying both verbally and visually.'

Rebecca looked at herself and realised she had let herself get caught out again wearing a mumsy, slightly shabby, should only be seen in the gym kind of outfit. Truth be told this wasn't really even good enough for the gym, her lilac windcheater was bordering on Nanna-ish. It was cheap and it was warm and she bought it when she was carrying Jacob, which meant it had to be, oh no, over seven years old. Not a smart message for a newly employed woman.

Louise and Cynthia were both confused at what they had done wrong. Louise looked smart, or so Cynthia had told her, so what was she doing wrong.

'All right Joy, what gives, exactly what is wrong with the way I look today!'

'You said it!'

'I said what?' Louise knew she was not sounding exactly friendly but she was feeling rattled and apparently it was starting to show. Through all of this Cynthia was sitting there chewing the quick of one of her nails in confusion, Rebecca stayed quiet looking from Louise to Joy, and Louise was on one of her rides. So the girls knew to stay clear.

'Tell me Joy what exactly did I say or do? You are not making sense today and I need help not more questions.'

'What other question is bothering you Luv,' asked Joy in a very kindly tone. She had picked up quickly that something was on Louise's mind and wanted to lay that dragon to rest before she continued with the other two girls. Immediately, Louise flashed her eyes at Joy, then in an instant her shoulders sagged and she let out a huge sigh.

'It's Tom!'

'What about Tom?' asked Joy.

'I knew it, that bastard has another family or is he running around with a younger woman. Men you can't trust the lot of 'em. You know I ...'

'Cynthia, let Louise finish,' interrupted Joy, her eyes as warm as the coffee in their hands and her tone soft like a mother.

'He has invited me to the Grand Final lunch at the Docklands and then he wants us to go away for the weekend up to Daylesford to the spas.'

'And your problem is?' interjected Cynthia. 'How marvellous. That lunch is so much fun, the women have lunch in one room with the men in another. Then the men come and join the women after lunch and a whole evening of merry making follows. But hang on who are you going with?'

'Apparently I am going with his friends' wives and girlfriends. The WAG set. This is too much. You know how I feel about crowds. I haven't met these women and I have to spend an afternoon with them. Then we are all going away together!' All together the girls all raised their eyebrows together, Joy included. Louise took a breath and continued.

'Yes together. Apparently a bus is picking us up later that evening. What if I don't like them, what will we talk about? What do I have to wear?' The girls didn't know whether to laugh or cry with Louise. Apparently from her comments she had no concerns about sleeping with Tom, it was her wardrobe she was confused about. As they looked at Louise's face it was Rebecca who started to find she could not hold her giggles in which led to Cynthia and Joy all bursting out into loud welcoming laughter. The only sort of laughter you can have with friends. Looking at her friends Louise found herself laughing with them as well. She knew she sounded ridiculous but there was nothing sacred nor was there any subject too ridiculous when it came to being with these women.

'So Joy, help me,' came Louise's heartfelt plea.

'Ladies listen up. Today we are going to work on the messages you are giving. Louise, did you realise when you get nervous you hide it behind an aggressive nature. How long have you been nervous about Tom's weekend away?'

'Since Saturday.'

'And let me guess you have been talking over everyone ever since?'

'No, not at all. Have I?' Louise looked at Rebecca and Cynthia for their response. They simply shrugged their shoulders. they hadn't spoken to Louise all week.

Joy continued. 'Let me put it to you this way. Have people been overly responsive to you this week?'

Before answering Louise mulled over her past week. 'No in fact I have been trying to find a part time job and have gotten nowhere.'

'No surprises there. But I can help you with that. Your survival mechanism is one that when you are in unfamiliar territory you become defensive and it shows as aggressive or antagonistic communication. So it doesn't matter how great you look. You sound short and sharp and will put anyone off. Your external and your internal messages are mixed. A mixed message will frighten anyone away. Lucky for Tom he was the cause of this aggression and as such is probably completely void of any awareness.' Joy was pleased to find the root of Louise's problem so quickly. She had come so far it would be a pity to see Louise shut down again.

Louise looked up at Joy, wearing her heart and her fear on her sleeve. 'So what do I do?'

Joy knew what she needed. 'You need to recognise this as a trait and re-adjust yourself and your language when you feel yourself becoming tense.'

'But what am I going to wear?' Back to the original problem. Which for many would be not so disaterous, Louise led the conversation.

'We'll get to that soon. I want to talk to Rebecca and Cynthia first.' Relieved Louise sat back in her chair and enjoyed her coffee which had been placed in front of her.

'Rebecca dear tell us about this job you were telling Louise about when Cyclone Cynthia entered.' Rebecca then filled the girls in on how she had seen the in-store demonstrator working at her local supermarket and how after calling around a couple of agencies she found one that focused primarily on food demonstrating. She didn't want to go to a promotions agency. There she would have been competing against the nineteen year olds fresh out of school who are ideal working as pit girls at the Grand Prix and look amazing in skimpy outfits. She wanted to be somewhere where the focus was on great service not a fabulous physique. As they listened the women nodded their heads as they could see how ideal this line of work was for someone like Rebecca who loved people, loved cooking and loved her kids. She had the best of both worlds.

Joy kept the conversation moving. 'So Rebecca, how keen are you on this work?'

'I love it. I have so much fun. I'm meeting people, I'm making money and I am home for the boys when they finish school.'

'Is it enough for you?' Gently Joy asked.

'I'll be honest. For now it is good but I wouldn't mind, sort of, you know, getting further. But that, well, sort of, you know, depends on so much and really, well it is kind of okay for what it is.'

'Oh my goodness stand up for yourself. Rebecca you have been with your children too long.' This came from Louise who whilst she had been chastised earlier knew that she was in a safe place to speak her mind.

'Louise is right Rebecca,' continued Joy. 'When it comes to you rejoining the workforce you have lost your spice. Louise has on the other hand too much spice. Women will love you in the store as you will be one of them but if you want to go further, even if it is down the road after the boys have finished primary school then you will have to lose the girly speak and start to say what you mean. Have you ever heard a male say kind of, sort of, just a thought?'

Rebecca put her head to the side in thought and remarkably Louise and Cynthia too fell deep in thought over Joy's question. She was right. Women have a habit of softening their speech to allow for fault or to sound as if they are making a suggestion rather than making a comment or a motion to proceed. While men take off at full throttle women will often proceed with caution.

'I do, don't I?' said Rebecca in a whisper voice, she hung her head and looked up at the women from her bowed head. Talk about channelling her inner Princess Di from the 1980s.

'Yes you do,' finished Joy for her. 'So I have a little task for you this week. Firstly speak with conviction. You will, you do and you are. No sort ofs or kind ofs and I don't want you to have a little idea. It is an idea or it is not. You decide. It is time to assert yourself again. I can see you running a team of those women in the future not just being one of the worker bees. Does that appeal to you?'

Rebecca's mouth went down at one side as she contemplated what Joy had said and it was as if that same part of her brain that had been reawakened when she realised she could start becoming her own person again had opened up further. 'Sure, I think I can? No I mean I will Joy. Thank you. That's exactly what I want to do.'

'Don't thank me, just do it.' It was Rebecca's turn to sit back in her chair and mull over what had been said to her today. As she sat back all eyes turned to Cynthia who was still trying to work out where she had gone wrong.

'Cyclone Cynthia, what are we to do with you?' started Joy. 'Have you listened to anything we have discussed up until now?'

Cynthia looked at Joy in confusion. 'I thought I was doing exactly as we had discussed. I am dressing for my body shape, my personality and I am working on my goals.'

'Which goals are those dear?'

'To get a promotion. I am getting more involved at work. Okay so I had a night out last night but it is only one and I had a very civil lunch date earlier this week with a gorgeous man. Remember the guy from the club who went home; well he came into work to see me and we went out for lunch. It was fantastic, I've been dying to tell you this. He came into work and waited for me, we chatted and then he took me out for lunch this week. It was all very proper and we are going to have lunch again next week. I don't know why he won't catch up with me at night but this is something different and it certainly is fun.'

'Tell me, were you late back to work after any of these lunch dates?' Joy looked at Cynthia knowingly.

'Yes but not by much and anyway no one will have noticed.' Cynthia still had no idea where Joy was heading.

'You don't think so. Have you received any promotions yet?'

'No, but ...' As Cynthia tried to finish what she had to say Joy cut her off.

'No buts about it. You are sending out mixed messages. You need to be more consistent. Firstly it sounds like you had a great couple of weeks dressing properly but then you let yourself down by coming and going at your own whim. Then it sounds like you have not just been getting involved but gossiping all over the office. It is one thing for someone to tell you information but it is another to be spreading it. Your bosses need to know you are reliable and the soul of discretion. Gabbling on as you do makes you appear like a brattish two year old. You know how adults react when children get out of control. We tune them out. My dear, that is what you are doing. Your constant ramblings are stopping your bosses from listening to the good stuff you have to say. You have fences to mend here for them to consider you and at this point in time you are still not reliable enough for them to consider you for any promotion. I am sure they love having you in the office but as to promoting you if they were looking at you today's effort in all likelihood has closed that book.'

'Do you really think so?' Cynthia had to ask. Joy's comments had caught Cynthia off guard. She didn't feel so sure of herself now.

Joy didn't leave it there. 'Well I don't know so but it is a possibility. You said it was a work meeting and you went in looking like the good time girl. What happened to those lovely clothes you were wearing the past weeks?'

'Oh I am still wearing them only today I didn't get home.' Cynthia answered lamely.

'Not good enough. You are either serious about your job or not. It is time you started becoming serious about that list you brought in after our first session. From here on in you will be not just on time but at least ten minutes early. I want you to stop repeating gossip and I want you to make sure you dress in the manner of which you want them to see you. If you want to remain the good time girl then stick with your boots and minis but if you want to be a serious contender for any promotions then this can't happen again. I make no apologies for sounding like a school mistress but I really want you to achieve all of the goals that you set out to achieve when we first got together. Can you do that?' Joy took a breath and leaned in toward Cynthia.

'Yes Ma'am.' Cynthia knew she had been chastised but it didn't feel wrong. It felt right and she felt that she was closer to her goals than ever in the past.

'Joy,' interrupted Louise, 'if you have finished with Cynthia we still haven't focused on what I need to wear and do for this weekend. At this point Cynthia started squirming around in her seat and looked at Joy and Louise with anticipation.

'I can help. Please let me,' Cynthia burst out.

'She's right, you know. Louise you should let Cynthia help you. She knows what is in your wardrobe better than I do and as long as she doesn't get you running around in miniskirts and tights I can't think of anyone better to help you.'

The idea of Cynthia dressing and preparing her wardrobe made Louise a little nervous. She would have been more comfortable getting Rebecca to help but then she may have found herself emulating Rebecca again. The girls decided to meet at Louise's on Saturday and then spend the afternoon shopping for whatever was missing. The rest of the time they chatted amongst themselves as Rebecca made sure she spoke up for herself, Louise didn't speak up so much and Cynthia just enjoyed the amicable gossip amongst her friends. After all this wasn't work and she could always say what she wanted to her friends.

Chapter 11.

Getting dressed

Getting dressed

The clatter of heels approaching her front door alerted Louise that Cynthia was on her way. She quickly finished wiping her kitchen benches, looked around her lounge and dining room to check she had put her magazines and papers away and went to the door. Cynthia was standing at the front door in her jeans, a striped tee, layers of chains around her neck and her purple boots. She had two takeaway coffees in her hand and a couple of muffins from the coffee shop down the road. Her face looked fresh. Even though it was clear to Louise she had make-up on she was obviously going for a low key look this morning, or as low key as Cynthia could create.

'Good morning Cinderella, are you ready for your fairy godmother to get you ready for the ball?'

'Oh, I'm not that bad surely, come on in. What have you got there?'

'Coffee to wake us up and choc chip muffins which I was assured are entirely low joule and fat free. Just what we need to handle this task to prepare you for the ball. Or shall we say the lunch and weekend away. Come on let's eat these muffins. I am famished and just a teensy bit hung over. I went out last night with the girls from work.'

'Will you ever settle down?'

'Sure, when there is someone to settle with. You'll be proud of me. I was home by 2am so it wasn't a late one. Anyway I'm here and today is all about you.' Cynthia starts looking around. 'I was hoping to meet the totally terrific Tom. Is he here?'

'Stop it. As if I would let Tom anywhere near you just yet. You'll scare him off. I can't have him thinking that I am hiding another side to me until he gets to know me much better.'

'Pity. I would have loved to check out Mr Tall Dark and Handsome.' As the girls enjoyed their easy banter, coffee and muffins there was a knock at the door. They looked at each other in surprise.

'I bet it's the kid from over the road coming to see if I want my lawns mowed. With Rob gone I am happier for him to earn his $15 and save me the hassle of dragging the lawn mower around the front and back yards.' Louise disappeared in the direction of the front door as Cynthia picked at her muffin. It was no wonder she was as thin as she was as she had a habit of picking at her food as opposed to shovelling it into her mouth. There was something very delicate about Cynthia's eating. That was about the only delicate thing about her though. Moments later Louise came back up the hall with the sound of a second pair of feet behind her.

'Good morning,' came a lilting sing song voice that Cynthia recognised as well as the sound of her own.

'Becs what are you doing here. How fabulous to see you. Where are the boys?' The last comment was accompanied with a manic head swivelling motion by Cynthia who loved the boys but knew they were a handful and wanted to make sure she was firmly seated on her bar stool before she got pushed in the rush of their affection.

'The boys are with Justin. They are playing an away game and as they are playing at the same field Justin has taken them. So I have a day off and I couldn't let you have all of the fun now could I? Ooh muffins, are there any left?' Rebecca then helped herself to a sneaky bite of Cynthia's muffin and went to the kettle to make herself a cup of tea. She had her own herbal tea bag in her handbag. She had stopped drinking coffee and was having only herbal teas which had also helped her in her quest to lose weight. 'So what have you decided girls?'

'We haven't started yet, have we Lou?'

'No,' came a slightly strangled cry from Lou who was still as nervous as a cat about this upcoming weekend.

'Okay, tell us again in detail exactly what the plans are.'

Louise then proceeded to outline the events as she knew them. Friday was the Grand Final Lunch. It was a dressy affair to which only the ladies attended at the grounds located down at the Docklands. After the lunch the men joined the women from their own lunch and from what she had heard it could become quite messy. This day they were going to have a few more drinks at the Docklands before they went to a booking Tom had made at Nobu at the Crown casino complex. After dinner a minibus was booked to come to Crown to take them all to a magnificent guesthouse up at Daylesford. The guesthouse slept eight and on the Saturday they were all going to the hot springs for a massage and mud bath. Saturday night they were going to have a local chef come in and cook for them in house so that they could lounge around the open fire and play games. This part Louise was still unclear about. She really hoped they meant board games but Cynthia was certain it was the car keys in a bucket kind of game where partner swapping was often the result. Rebecca joined in with Cynthia's ribbing until she could see Louise becoming noticeably nervous about the whole event. Before they completely freaked her out they agreed that quite likely it was something like Monopoly or cards. Something they could do to pass the time with as they enjoyed beautiful wines and got to know each other better. Cynthia remembered a past boyfriend who she used to play Mah-jong with him and his family every Saturday night down at their holiday house and drink port. To this day she still loved playing Mah-jong and even had a game on her iPhone which she played when she was stuck waiting for a meeting to begin.

Once Louise was settled again they asked about Sunday. Sunday was going to include a bush walk, a long lunch at the famous Lake House restaurant and then their bus would come to bring them back in time to be back in the city by 5pm.

'You know Louise if you don't want to go I will,' piped up Cynthia.

'Me too,' added Rebecca. This sounded like an ideal weekend to both girls, only Louise was out of sorts with it. She was becoming more of a home body as she got older.

'The way I see it Lou, you need seven outfits for this trip.'

'Cyn, there are only two whole days to cater for. Where do you get seven situations from?'

'Simple, you need something smashing for lunch slash dinner on Friday. Something to go to the hot springs in and something to wear to dinner that night. Then you have your bush walk the next morning and you have something smart and casual for lunch.'

'Unless you did different maths to me that only adds up to five outfits. You said seven.'

'Exactly! I am assuming, and correct me if I am wrong, that you will be sleeping with Tom and there is no way you are going to go to bed in that t-shirt and those flannelette pants I spied in your laundry before. Maybe you'll need something for two nights but then again maybe you'll need nothing at all but it is better to be prepared. Especially if they all go to breakfast or have coffee in their pyjamas in the morning.'

'Oh God, what have I got myself into. Why couldn't he just want to take me to the local Italian restaurant, fill me up on a bottle of cheap spumante and then ravish me in his lounge room? This is too much for me.'

'Come on Lou it is going to be fun. But hang on a minute, I have to get a few things out of my car for you.' As Cynthia ran outside Rebecca and Louise raised their eyebrows at each other. They had no idea what could come out of Cynthia's car. A moment later a chirpy Cynthia breezed back in pulling an overnight bag on wheels. It was a Spencer and Rutherford bag. These bags were absolutely stunning and something Louise had always admired. This one was shaped like a half moon hat box on wheels. It was decorated in shades of maroon and green with a lime zip. Very Cynthia. Nervously Louise wondered what the bag contained and held her breath.

'What's up? Don't you like it?'

'What's not to like. It's gorgeous but I am scared about what you have inside it.'

'Inside it? Why nothing. We are filling it with your clothes. I'm loaning it to you for the weekend. My guess is this crowd weekend a lot and I don't want you to look like the kid from school who is using an old back pack for the weekend. And if they all use old back packs then you will look stylish at least.'

Cynthia started to take the bag to Louise's bedroom to fill it and caught a look of relief wash over Louise's features.

'Hang on. Don't tell me you thought this bag contained my stuff. You dirty stop out. As if I'd be lending you my toys. That's just gross.' With that she pulled a face and continued down to the bedroom with the two girls in tow.

Over the next hour Rebecca and Cynthia went through Louise's wardrobe to find exactly what she would need. They agreed that she had to buy a dress for the lunch and that night rather than stuffing it into her case it could travel home in a suit bag. Her jeans would be suitable for going to the Spa in, and with that she could wear a cami with a shirt and her cream wool jacket. As they were staying in for dinner she could change into her cream wool pants with her red boots and they wanted her to wear her pleated tank top and charcoal grey cardigan also. They found a small pair of red earrings to complete the outfit. If they changed their mind and went out for dinner she could slip her cream wool jacket on top.

For Sunday they thought it would be okay to wear her jeans again as long as she wore them with a thicker jumper and flat walking shoes and then changed her shoes and top for lunch. Back into her red boots with a new turtleneck they decided and some great necklaces to funk up her look. Louise wasn't too sure if she wanted to be funked up but she did know she didn't want to look daggy.

All that was left now was to select her lingerie. Rebecca looked into her underwear drawer and gasped.

'Louise, you can't possibly be serious!'

'What? What's wrong? Get out of my knickers drawer will you.'

'Cyn, look at these.' And with that she held up a very large pair of very comfy beige undies which would have made Bridget Jones feel very much at home. Together the girls went into peals of laughter as they tossed the underwear between the two of them and out of Louise's reach until finally, exhausted from laughing the three of them fell into a heap on Louise's bed. Just like the old days.

'Lou, you know we cannot possibly allow you to go away without new underwear at the very least.'

'But who is going to see and anyway I'll get changed before Tom sees me in my undies.'

'That doesn't matter. Your underwear is your foundation and a pair of boggy knickers will give you a boggy air. You will know. That's how and you mark my words great underwear makes you feel fantastic. Do you think it takes great looks to be an amazing woman? No way. It takes great attitude, confidence and great foundations. And great foundations start with your underwear. You would be amazed if you knew the underwear some of the world's top leaders wear. Both men and women, but that is another story. It is the clothing closest to your body. You have to respect yourself enough to wear the best at least.'

'But I don't want to blow my budget on French lace knickers and anyway they make me scratch.'

'You don't have to get French lace but at least some quality microfibre will be miles better than what you have. Now are you a colours or a neutrals kind of girl. Personally I like colour and with that Cynthia revealed a flash of hot pink from just below the waist band of her jeans.'

'And I am a pastel lace girl,' as Rebecca lifted her skirt just enough to reveal the side of her lemon panties.

'You strike me as a neutrals kind of gal but that doesn't have to mean beige, beige and more beige.' Cynthia was in her element. She continued her colour education to a startled Louise. 'You need some fawn, not beige.'

'What's the difference?' asked a non-plussed Louise. Knickers were knickers weren't they? Well obviously not if you listened to Cynthia.

'Nothing really, but I hate the word beige it is so … beige,' finished Cynthia. 'As I was saying. Some fawn, a pair of black and maybe even some powder grey for when you want a hint of elegance to your appearance.'

'I just thought I was getting knickers not a whole emotional and spiritual resource centre.'

'Call them what you will but we are getting you new underwear. Come on girls, we have shopping to do.' It went without question that the girls would be helping Louise purchase a special something to wear to bed. Not too racy but not too normal either and a beautiful new robe. Her dressing gown was the same one she wore when she was nursing Jade. There was no way she could take it away with her. Frankly they were surprised if it would last the journey.

The whole shopping trip took the afternoon which left them time to enjoy a glass of wine at the end of the day. Time could have stood still as the three school friends giggled and laughed at the table only now they were drinking wine and not cokes. Louise had everything she needed including some new body lotion which was a gift from Rebecca and a packet of condoms which Cynthia hid in with her lingerie. A girl can never be too prepared she thought with a mischievous grin to herself.

'Here's to Louise getting away and getting laid,' announced Cynthia as she raised her glass. A chorus of 'hear, hear' followed from the others and much laughter. Whilst heads turned in the restaurant the girls were oblivious and many patrons were envious of the fun they were having.

Chapter 12.

Show your true colours

Show your true colours

As the sun peeked out from behind the grey clouds that signalled the end of winter, Cynthia flittered into the café as bright as any bird with exotic plumage. It appeared she had been listening to the advice from past weeks. Her skirts came to a very respectable length just below her knee and her boots, though high, were paired with an opaque tight so she was exuding a look which said class, not arse. Her top was a slightly fitted very fine cashmere knit. All in all the clothing was as Joy had been advising her on. The only item that did raise Joy's eyebrows as Cynthia entered was the fact she was wearing scarlet red. Yes she could and probably had stopped traffic during the day.

Joy was starting to worry if she would ever get the message through to Cynthia that she didn't have to try so hard. She was wonderful in her own right and did not need to over embellish what she already had. Hopefully today would take care of that for her.

The café was quiet and Joy was putting away the last of the lunch cups and saucers. In her mind she went back to the heady days of her own youth. She remembered the swinging sixties. Looking at Cynthia reminded her of the colour and the excitement that was dressing in the style immortalised by Mary Quant girls. Joy was only 18 when she travelled to London with William for their honeymoon. She was barely out of school and it was while she was shopping that she wandered into one of Mary Quant's Bazaar stores and was discovered. The look and the feel of the Mary Quant style had never been seen before. Miniskirts were not new but they were shorter and with the great tights Mary designed and her bright shoes, there was nothing subtle about her appearance. It was the bright colourful combinations that were put together. The importance of primary colours and the slick, angled bob which would give Posh Spice a real run for her money. Joy remembered fondly, being approached by Mary herself and being asked to model for an upcoming parade she had on. Her favourite outfit was a pair of hot pink hot pants and white ribbed turtleneck skivvy. She would wear her white tights and she had a pair of blue and white Mary Janes with a square toe and square heel. If she thought about it they could be quite nanna-ish if it wasn't for the entire colour. Mary had talked her into having her long blonde hair cropped short and dyed black for impact. It made her luminous blue eyes literally pop out of her head and eyes were all of the rage back then. The larger and more doe eyed a girl could look the more in fashion she was. Everyone wore fake eye lashes and looked lost in their photographs. When they weren't jumping around with oversized umbrellas. There was no concern for occupational health and safety then. It was nothing to do a photo shoot of you jumping from a tall ladder in an extraordinary high pair of heels. There were no padded mats to land on as they didn't have the tools to crop anything out of a photo or digitally enhance it. The most they could do was hand mask an area of the photo as it was hand developed. Those were heady days. Hanging out with the Beatles and a very young Mick Jagger. She never knew whose house she would be invited to or in those days exactly what might be in her coffee. After one very confusing weekend when she had been out with some of her modelling friends she had had her cup laced with LSD. That was her first and last time using drugs. They just didn't sit well with her so from there on she always preferred to make her own cup of tea. Many thought she was strange. She just knew she was protecting herself. LSD was rife among the modelling and rock and roll world and it was never Joy's cup of tea, to coin a phrase. What she did inherit from the sixties was a love of colour and a no-fear attitude for trying anything different when it came to food or lifestyles.

Here was Cynthia still looking as fresh at nearly forty as Joy felt at nineteen. She felt somewhat two faced as she was going to have to tell Cynthia to do as I say not as I do. However everyone wore psychedelic prints in the sixties but they certainly were not wearing them in corporate offices when they were trying to get a promotion. However, they may have had a fabulous beehive in place.

Her thoughts were interrupted by Louise coming through the doors, with a somewhat sheepish expression on her face. Joy could tell this newly single life was not necessarily the ideal life for Louise but she would have to get used to it. Anyway it sounded like Tom was pretty keen so she had little to worry about. Joy was just about to open her mouth to say hi as a barrage of questions hurtled at Louise from the flaming pink flamingo in the corner.

'Lou, Lou, tell us, how did IT go? So was the weekend perfect? Was Tom dreamy? What did you wear? Did you do what we told you to do? Were the girls nice? What was the spa like? The Lake House, was it a dream? I've heard the food is amazing. Come on spit it out, what's stopping you?'

'Cyn, settle down. I'll tell you what's stopping her and that's you!' Rebecca's breezy voice floated over Louise's head towards Cynthia. She had walked in just behind Louise but no one would have noticed her with the colour and noise emanating from Cynthia. It was as if a colourful macaw was chirping away in the corner.

'Cyn, what's with the galaxy of colours you are wearing today? From the waist down you look like a nun but from above you are a riot of colour.' Even Joy had failed to notice the wild earring swinging from Louise's lobes. Hiding under her hair it wasn't until she started calling out to Louise and bobbing her head around madly that they revealed themselves from beneath her sheath of blonde highlighted hair.

'I just felt like some colour in my life today. Everyone in the office is so dull. You would think that they didn't have any excitement in their lives. But enough about me ... for once. Lou tell us all about your weekend.'

Lou looked coy as she simply stated, 'It was nice.'

'What were the others like?' egged on Rebecca.

'They were nice too.'

'The place you stayed at in Daylesford?' put in Joy.

'Yeah, nice, no complaints.'

'Let me guess, sex with Tom was nice too,' finished Cynthia.

'Oh no, that was great, but the whole weekend was just so busy. We were either lunching, walking, spa-ing, drinking, eating or something. There was not a minute's peace.'

'You weren't at a commune. What did you expect?' Rebecca had a giggle to herself remembering some of the weekends away she had had and in many cases sleep was just an option. This weekend had sounded heavenly on so many levels to her. Cynthia shared her sentiments.

'I really don't know. When Rob and I would go away with the kids I had loads of time to myself to read, or cook or, I'm not too sure. Just time to myself.'

'Louise, my guess is they left you alone to do what they liked and left you to organise their meals. That is not what an adult weekend away is all about.' Rebecca had to add this piece, Louise's prior weekends sounded like work not relaxation.

'I can see that. It was different. Don't get me wrong I had a lovely time. I think I am still exhausted that's all. Cyn, I've got your case out in my car. I'll give it to you when we leave. By the way they were very impressed by all of the outfits which I had and in such a small stylish case. I am glad I borrowed it.'

'Glad to be of help. So Joy, what's it to be today? Elocution lessons, deportment? What does the house of Joy have in store for us?'

'Ladies this week we are going to focus on you and how each of you hides your true colours.'

'I don't think Cyn is hiding at all in her luminous, traffic stopping hot pink sweater with rainbow dayglo earrings.' Lou could not help but laugh at the spectacle of vibrancy Cynthia was assuming.

'Actually Louise, Cynthia is hiding herself even more than you or Rebecca is today. Just as I said last week that by being loud she is no longer being listened to at work ...'

Before Joy could finish Cynthia butted in to her sentence. 'And you will be pleased to know I have not gossiped once in the past week. So if I start babbling to you at the end of our session with Joy I am apologising now because I didn't realise how often I did. But I have curbed that bad habit.'

'Perfect Cynthia but I am afraid your clothing is now making the noise for you.'

'What do I have to do? Become a monk. Maybe I'll just start wearing saffron robes everywhere or, I know, black, black and more black and blend in with the masses in the city. I'll just be another ant walking up Collins Street to work every day.' Cynthia fell back into her seat feeling defeated.

'What if I told you that by wearing the right colours you will stand out from the crowds in a way you never have before?' Joy quizzically raised her eyebrow to Cynthia as she issued her with what could almost be considered a challenge.

Cynthia in no mood to be picked on asked. 'In a good way or am I going to get shot down again?'

'Have I ever shot you down?' Joy could sense Cynthia was at a low spot so she softened her aim.

'No, but I think you've had me in your sights.' Cynthia rsponded.

'Cynthia, you've got it all wrong. You can be loud, but no one has heard you, you can be obvious and no one has seen you. I want you to be real and no one will miss you.'

'Wow', all three girls sat back into their seats and looked at Joy as if she was a wise guru.

'How did you ever get to be so wise? I can't wait until I grow up and people start listening to me,' mused Cynthia.

'Cynthia, the only thing age has given me is wrinkles and liver spots. Listening gave me wisdom. Don't put yourself down. You will be amazed at what you can do if you put your mind to it.'

Cynthia rubbed her hands together effecting an evil magician and said, 'imagine what I could do if I used my mind for good instead of evil, he he he'. Joy threw her one of her looks. 'Sorry Joy, couldn't help myself,' said Cynthia as she sat on her hands so they wouldn't get her into any more trouble.

'You girls will be the end of me I swear.' Joy smiled at all the girls so that they could resettle and refocus on today's task. 'Colour. Today we are going to look at the choices we make in colour and why we do so. Colour says so much about who we are and how we are feeling. It speaks to everyone around us as sure as if you were speaking aloud. Or in Cynthia's case squawking at everyone.' The girls enjoyed the little digs at Cynthia as they knew Joy did not have a mean bone in her body and was only messing with them.

'Have a look around the café here and see what I have done with colour. Rebecca, can you describe the other end of the bar for me please?'

'Well I can see your staff. They are wearing black pants and a milk coffee coloured shirt with darker stripes on them and your logo is down the arms which gives the bar a funky but not too formal appearance. Your booths are in shades of cream and rich chocolate brown and you have deep red light fittings which I know glow warmly at night and during the day give a spark of colour to the room. Overall it is a very warm and welcoming feeling.'

'Nice description and spot on. I have used the creams and browns to make it easy for everyone to both blend in and feel at home here. The black pants are simply because anyone working in hospitality has black pants and it means I don't have to get them to buy anything else, but the shirts are so that they appear warm and friendly. The red lamps create a feeling of warmth and passion, especially at night. Not that I want this to be a pick up joint but if a young couple want to come here for a date it will inspire romance and hopefully a bit of an appetite. Have you noticed how Italian restaurants use red tablecloths? That gets the appetite going and the blood flowing and makes people want to eat more. They are not silly. So what do you think if I placed some vases with electric blue lilies in them or added some icy pink roses into the mix?' One the girls said 'uggh'.

'Why did you do that Cynthia?'

'Well for a start the room looks so warm and welcoming and adding those colours in would clash with the mood and harmony you have down there. Even the paintings you have on the wall are in those similar earthy tones.'

'So tell me, Cynthia, why have you chosen to clash with your natural décor?'

'I don't get what you are asking me. I'm not at home.'

'I'm talking about your own personal colouring. Let's break down your colouring as if we were describing a room. Are you okay with that?'

'You know me if it is about me then I am okay.' Cynthia was back on track and ready to receive again.

'Alright, your skin has a soft peachiness to it. Your eyes are a medium teal blue not a vibrant cobalt blue, which if they were would harmonise perfectly with your jumper and your hair is, and I say this with love remember, is a light mousey brown which you have highlighted blonde. All over your colouring is soft, muted and warm, and the difference in colour from your eyes to your hair to your skin is of a medium intensity. That is they are no more than 2–4 shades apart. If you think of white being 1 and black being 10 then you are ranging from a 3–7 in colour depth. So with this in mind, you should be wearing clothing which has a medium intensity to it. Your outfit is very high, in fact it is screaming so to make it work you have had to add very heavy eye colour to create a balance in your appearance. How would you look without your eye make-up on?'

'Oh, I'd look like shit basically.'

'So why are you hiding your beauty, your natural beauty behind such bright colour and make-up?'

'I don't know, I love these colours.' Cynthia looked to Rebecca and Louise for support but their faces told her that they agreed with Joy.

'I think you'll find you enjoy hiding behind those colours. Look if you really love wearing the bright colours and I must say I think your personality carries those colours perfectly, then I would rather you wore them as accessories not primaries to your outfit. What do you say spending a week toning down the volume on your wardrobe. I want you to look for colours which will make you look amazing without make-up on. Then apply your make-up. See what the difference is? I want you to think, warm and muted, a little smokey. You will be amazed at how intriguing your look can be.'

'Ooh, I've never been considered intriguing before. You're on Joy. This is exciting. Anyway it's time for a change. I've been doing this look for the past year and it hasn't worked so I'm happy to try something new.' Cynthia smiled and looked off into space as she started mentally planning her new wardrobe colours.

'Okay Rebecca, what is going on with you today?'

'I thought I looked quite nice! I've got on well fitting pants like you said, cute flats, I'm out of my runners and this little pale pink top that I picked up last week. It has a v-neck so I don't look all bosomy and floats over my middle so the remains of what the boys did to me are secreted away. As you say I am showing off my good assets. What should I have done?'

'Rebecca your clothes are perfect but your contrast level is all wrong. You are disappearing on us. Let's really look at you shall we?'

'If we must. Go for it Joy.' Rebecca was enjoying rediscovering her image and how it good it felt to be visible again.

'Your skin is like porcelain, you are very cool and clear. Your eyes however are deep brown and your hair is also very dark. You could wear the bright top that Cynthia has on quite well.'

'All right Cyn, take your top off it's mine.'

'Hang on a minute, I can't wear that soft pink you are wearing it's not muted enough for me. Is that right Joy?'

'Well done, Cynthia, you are very quick to learn.'

'Rebecca, aside from the fact I don't exactly want a fashion disrobing going on here at the café Cynthia is right, the top you are wearing is not for her. It is good for you but you have to dial up your contrast. I'd love to see a dark camisole under your top to give you some contrast or some jewellery to create the right level of higher contrast on you. You need to wear clothes and colours that have definite levels of light and dark in them to highlight your face.'

'Wait a minute, this might help.' Out of her bag she pulled a strand of deep blue beads that one of the boys had made into a necklace for her at school. She had forgotten they were at the bottom of her rather large handbag. In an instant she had attached the rope around her neck with a small bow and the effect was instantaneous. Her eyes glittered and her face was illuminated.

'Jacob told me they reminded him of my eyes. I never thought he was onto something.'

'You would be amazed at what children notice. That son of yours has quite an eye for colour. Take him shopping with you. He could be a designer or stylist in the making.' Joy was impressed with Jacob's choice for his mother and truly meant her comments.

'Now Louise, tell me about your outfit.'

'I think I've got what you are talking about regarding colour from an earlier session we had. I look for nature and it seems to flatter me. I've given away all of the pretty pinks and blues in my wardrobe. Today I'm just relaxing in this avocado green shirt with brown pants. Don't tell me I need more colour please. I feel really comfortable in all of this.'

'Actually Louise I thought you looked remarkable. The colours suit your warm complexion. Your skin is warm beige, your eyes are a medium green and your hair is a light umber. So all in all you will look best in medium contrast. You are neither too light nor too dark. In the words of Red Riding Hood you are just right. Keep it up. When you wear anything close in tone to your skin though try and wear a jacket or jewellery the colour or intensity of your eyes and you'll balance yourself out.' Louise breathed a sigh of relief. After the gruelling couple of weeks if not months she had had updating her image she just wanted to be on the right track for once and it sounded like she was. Finally it was all coming together. Now if she could just find some work everything would be perfect for her.

'So my little chickens. You are almost to the end of your journey. I can see big changes in each of you.'

'What's next?' asked Cynthia.

'Ah, that is for you to wait and see. I want each of you to pull together everything we have talked about over the past six sessions and see what changes can occur in your lives in the next fortnight. I think you'll be amazed. Now I must excuse myself I have some work to do. See you all next time.' With that Joy moved to the other end of the bar and fell into a deep conversation with her staff.

The girls spent another hour together grilling Louise on the nitty gritty details of her weekend away before they too all went their own ways for now.

Chapter 13.

Is that really you?

Is that really you?

That weekend the girls had agreed to all attend the gallery opening of a friend of Joy's. His name was Sergei Komarnitskaia and everyone just called him Sergei Sky. He was a Russian artist who had arrived in Melbourne in the 1950s and remained part of an art underground movement. Why they had remained underground for all of these years amazed everyone. Coming from Russia they had known a different life to many and did not want to lose what they had. Even though the Cold War had officially been over since 1991, Sergei acted like it was still strong and the KGB was around the corner. His art on the other hand was light and fluid. There was a delicacy of touch and colour that felt as if the hand of an angel had painted his works. Sergei had that strong Baltic look, penetrating eyes, square jaw, square forehead, straight nose and fine lips. It was just the smattering of grey in his blonde hair and the fine lines around his eyes that belied his age which was closing in on seventy now. There must have been something in that vodka he consumed more religiously than coffee or tea. One could easily imagine him standing with a military rifle slung casually over his shoulder and marching the streets, so where this work sprung from was anyone's guess. He had developed such a strong following over the decades that much of his work was now sold before it was finished and graced the walls of private collections all over the globe. This exhibition was both a retrospective of his own work and a chance for Sergei to come out from behind his self imposed prison and expose the younger artists he had discovered along the way to the world.

Joy had invited the girls before they left the café the last time they were together and she had asked each of them to bring a date. This was really unusual as they had never done anything as a group before. Well with Joy that was, and why would she insist on them bringing someone? It was not as if they were attending a wedding or was it that she was nervous that Sergei would not get the required numbers and would require room fillers. Rebecca would obviously bring Justin and Louise would bring Tom, which had Cynthia salivating like a love struck school girl. What was it with Cynthia and tradesmen? But who would Cynthia bring? She could call Phil but she hadn't seen him in ages and anyway she was completely over him. She thought of asking Mike but would he come? They had started meeting regularly, well if you could call once a week for lunch regular. She enjoyed his company and he was a nice guy but she hadn't worked out yet if he had a girlfriend or not. He never mentioned anyone but then he kept changing the subject when she asked him. Oh hell, why not, he could only say no and it wasn't as if she was inviting him to her house and to bed.

One by one the girls arrived at the gallery. Rebecca strolled in first looking absolutely stunning in a pair of navy bootleg pants, a blue and white striped top and a below the hip red trench. Her hair was out of its restraining ponytail and bouncing down her back. She had applied more make-up than usual which complimented her complexion. She had lined her eyes in charcoal and filled her lips in with fire engine red. It was the sort of red every woman aspires to but only a few can wear. Justin stood beside her looking incredibly handsome and exceptionally proud of his wife. He had always loved her, that was never a concern, but he had become concerned that she was no longer caring for herself. He knew the boys were hard work but he hadn't known what he could do or how he could help her. Whatever this Joy had done for her he wanted to give her a big kiss for he had brought his bubbly gorgeous Rebecca back to him. More than that he had brought her back to her. She was alive again. There was that impish grin hiding in her eyes again and you could see that she was thinking again. She was focusing on more than just what had to be done to get through the day and get everyone in the house fed, clothed, cleaned and out of the door. They picked up a glass of wine each and strolled around the gallery. They enjoyed their time alone in each other's company until the others arrived. They had always been happy in their own space.

About ten minutes later Louise and Tom arrived. Louise looked fabulous in a pair of charcoal straight leg pants, a cream camisole and a jacket with a soft animal print in beige, bone and darkest brown. In her ears she had a pair of amber studs and a piece of lopsided amber on a piece of silk around her neck. Tom looked ruggedly handsome in his RM Williams boots, pale moleskin trousers and his blue and white striped heavy cotton shirt. He could have walked straight off an urban bushman's catalogue page. He held the door open for Louise as they entered and his blue eyes danced merrily as he surveyed the room they entered. Louise saw Rebecca with Justin immediately and led Tom over to her friends. There was no awkwardness in their introductions and once Louise and Tom had a drink in their hands an easy flowing conversation followed.

The girls were starting to worry about Cynthia for while she was always erratic and prone to being late to work they generally found her to be quite timely when it came to social events. They had been talking for about half an hour when Cynthia and a stranger slipped through the doors. This was a Cynthia they had never seen before. Gone were the psychedelic colours. In their place was a vision of beauty. She had had some low lights put into her blonde hair so that it shimmered rather than had a brassy finish. Not that her hair ever looked brassy but with the amount of highlighting she had had through her hair there was little natural left and the colour required toning so often to keep it looking healthy. She was wearing a wool sheath dress reminiscent of the 1940s. This dress hugged her shape and created a silhouette of a waist from the creative use of stitching lines. It was in a dove grey and she accessorised it with a plum clutch and plum bob earrings. She had on sheer hosiery and a pair of fantastic mid grey suede court shoes with the squared off toes that looked as if a ballerina could go onto Pointe in them. She was elegance personified and she had even had her hair styled into a 1940s chignon. Once Rebecca and Louise had gotten over the impact of her appearance they then locked eyes on her escort. He was tall, nice looking, even somewhat safe looking. He wasn't ruggedly manly as in Tom's case, nor was he boyishly handsome as in Justin's case. He was nice looking. He had on a pair of dark trousers, plain shirt and a black velour jacket. Smart looking but in a very quiet sort of way. The girls all waved at each other and threaded their way through the crowd to meet up on the side of the room and make introductions.

'Becs, Louise, Justin and you must be Tom. Hi, I'm Cynthia and this is Mike.'

The conversation was centring around how the girls knew each other, how they had gone to school together and then like vultures the girls singled out each male to find out how he fitted into the picture.

Justin was so pleased he had known the girls as long as he had so he was excused from the where did you meet and what do you do line of questioning. He led the men into safe topics of sports and cars while the girls continued talking amongst themselves.

It was when Louise was returning from the bathroom that she spied a very small piece hiding in a corner of the gallery. She knew Tom was now speaking with another one of his friends he had bumped into, Cynthia and Mike were doing their own round of the canvases and Rebecca and Justin were talking to Joy so she had a moment to inspect this little treasure.

'I see you are inspecting one of my favourites. What do you see in this image? What does it make you feel?' A distinctly Russian voice spoke quietly into her ear as Louise was bending to look into the artwork. Louise bounced up, feeling as if she had been caught red handed with her hand in the lolly jar. She went bright red as she locked eyes with the bluest eyes she had ever seen in her life.

'I ... well I was ... it is, um ... oh you must be Sergei! I'm Louise I am a friend of Joy's. Thank you for inviting me. This piece is brilliant. How did you manage to catch that thread of light in the corner of the image? It has the glow of a Turner without the heaviness of the landscape.'

'Ah you can see the light. Many people today they do not see the light inside the picture. They will simply see that it is a landscape and walk on. I see you have an eye for art. You are an artist ... ya?'

'An artist, me? No. I like painting but I am not an artist. Oh I wish I could paint more than I do. I love to dabble and it is my favourite hobby, but that is all. At the moment I'm not doing anything until I get a job. I don't get it. I've been looking everywhere, you see I love gardening and have gone to all of the local nurseries but no one is hiring. It's that blasted drought. Everyone is too scared that they will be closed soon. Most nurseries are specialising in water tanks and not gardens now and I appear too unemployable.' Without realising, Louise spent the next forty minutes talking to Sergei about art, life, how Rob left her and the world in general. She was witty and fun, she wasn't all doom and gloom and Sergei enjoyed her company immensely. She too felt safe talking to Sergei. It was not as if a seventy year old was going to try and pick her up and his talent and love of life was infectious. She knew where his delicacy of touch came from. It came from within his soul. She was sure of that.

'So you come here Monday morning. Ya?'

'Monday morning? I don't understand.'

'I am offering you job. I need gallery manager and you need job. You can see inside my work so you will be good to help me and the artists I train. You see with your soul not your eyes. You are perfect. Now you go back to your friends. Ya. Until Monday Louise.' With that Sergei sauntered back to his circle of Russian expats, and joined in on their merry conversation.

Louise found Tom talking to a few of his friends and joined him for another drink and then she gathered the girls to tell them her astonishing news. Rebecca and Cynthia were ecstatic for Louise, and Joy, when she heard, just smiled quietly to herself. It was as if she knew Louise would be offered the job.

The night had been a huge success for Sergei, for the artists and for the girls. Rebecca felt alive again; Louise was excited about the prospect of not just a job but living her dream of being around artists. She had thought Joy was referring to a blooming garden not the blooming of her heart and soul through art. Cynthia was having a wonderful evening with Mike. He was warm, he was attentive, he wasn't rushing her, he got along with her friends, he laughed at her jokes. Hang on didn't they all in the beginning. Well, that aside, he made her feel special and she didn't feel she had to put on some show to keep him interested. After the gallery they went into the city to the Oyster Bar and had a supper of oysters and a glass of a velvety smooth sauvignon blanc after which he dropped her home. He then left but not before he gently kissed her good night at her front door and promised to call her the next day.

Back upstairs above her café, where Joy lived she too was settling down for the night. Everything was working perfectly for her. Tonight had been perfect. Sergei and Louise had met and discovered that they were perfect for each other. Not in a sexual way but as a mentor and student, only they didn't know it yet. He thought that Louise was just going to manage his studio but Joy knew that in time Sergei would unleash the inner talent hiding in Louise.

Rebecca had rediscovered herself. Her job was giving her a purpose to get up every day again more so than just taking care of her house and you could see that she and Justin were as much in love as ever. She had better be careful or there may be a daughter on her horizon if she didn't watch out. That would be up to fate though and she never interfered with fate.

Finally Cynthia was getting the message. She looked absolutely stunning tonight. She had removed all of her extra stuff and allowed her own light to shine through. Mike had seemed a nice boy too. Time alone would tell.

Joy picked up the picture of William she had sitting beside her bed.

'I miss you sweetheart, but I'm in no hurry to see you. So you'll just have to wait for me my dear.' Joy then lightly kissed the frame and slid into bed and turned out her light.

Chapter 14.

Working wardrobes

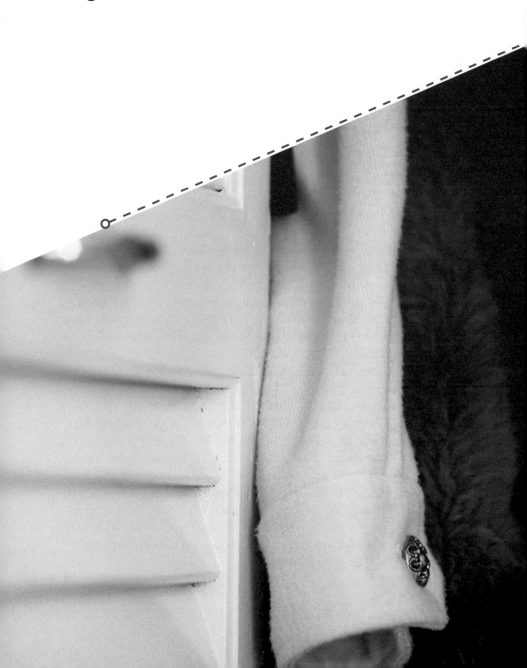

Working wardrobes

Thursday arrived and the girls were all early. There was something special about today but they didn't know what it was. It had only been five days since the weekend but they all felt as if so many changes were at play in their lives and they didn't know what to focus on or talk about first. So until Joy came to join them the noise from their corner of the café was a cacophony of voices with no discernable words filtering out of their huddle. To an onlooker it would look as if everyone was speaking over everyone else but they were completely aware of all that was being said and the responses that were being formed.

Joy finished serving the last customer, handed over to her afternoon shift employee and joined the girls sitting at their booth.

'Well, well, well. Look at the three of you. Who would've thought that you were the same three women I first sat down with almost four months ago?'

Cynthia piped up, 'We know. But guess what, I can't believe I am saying this. We have some good news and some bad news for you. Joy, you know those goals you had us fill in, well they are coming true.'

'How so? Tell me everything because it sounds as if my work is finished with the three of you.' The girls all looked quickly to each other as they hadn't considered that Joy would know what they were going to say.

'I have a promotion. Which is fabulous and shit all at once.' Cynthia was beaming frm ear to ear.

'Cynthia that is fantastic news! I am so pleased for you. You have worked really hard at this I know. But I thought you wanted a promotion. Why do you after all of this time say it is shit?'

'Well my boss sat me down only yesterday. You see I was having my annual performance appraisal and said they had noticed how hard I had been working on my image at work and thought I was ready to have my own clients. Which is just fantastic but I have to give up my flexi day for this new position so I can no longer pop in here Thursday afternoons. And to add to that, I've been buying a new outfit nearly every week and I can't keep doing that.'

'Cynthia, we always knew this was going to be for only as long as it was needed. Don't worry I think I can help you cut down on what you are spending but give you more clothes than you ever had before. Louise, let me guess, you are required at the gallery as well.'

'I'm lucky in that the gallery is only open five days a week but that is Wednesday to Sunday so Thursdays were going to be a problem for me as well. We also open by appointment on Monday and Tuesday for some of Sergei's special clients. Had you said anything Joy as Sergei told me he didn't need me today?'

'Sergei is a dear old friend of mine and I might have said something about you coming here today. I do hope he is still paying you for a full week though, as I didn't want him to dock your wages for me. Believe me he can afford it.'

'He wanted to but I wouldn't hear of it.' Louise didn't want anything to unsettle the happiness she had at her new job and feeling like she was getting favours she didn't deserve was not the way to begin.

'Well ladies. Let's get working on your problems as it sounds as if this is your final session with me. I do hope you'll keep coming back though.'

'Oh we will Joy, you can't get rid of us that easily,' Rebecca said for all of the girls.

'Focus ladies, where were we? Cynthia let's start planning your work wardrobe.'

'Planning!! I've never planned a wardrobe in my life. I buy outfits and loads of them. Every outfit is spectacular and every outfit is individual and completely unrelated to any other outfit in my wardrobe.'

'So let me guess you have a wardrobe full or orphans who bear little to no resemblance to the piece next to them and rather than having a social melting pot you are having identity conflicts.'

'You could say that,' returned Cynthia, a small furrow forming between her brows.

'I don't have that problem, mine is that my clothes are all nice but none are exceptional enough to be seen in a gallery. How am I, a relaxed personality meant to look gallery fabulous every day, enough for Sergei and the sort of person he attracts to him? I'm just going to let him down and he is going to regret every having asked me to manage his gallery,' finished Louise with a long deep sigh.

'Are we experiencing a wardrobe epidemic of catastrophic proportions because that is my problem too.' The girls all looked at Rebecca.

'I'm losing weight and nothing fits me but I am scared if I spend too much money now and I lose more weight I'll not be able to wear these clothes soon and then I will have wasted all of that money. I want to look good and I need to for work but I don't know what to do either.' Rebecca looked at the girls smiling at her and realised hers was a problem many women would love to have but it was still a problem to be dealt with.

'So ladies, let me ask you. Is this the worst problem you have right now?' Joy asked. Louise and Cynthia nodded their heads but Rebecca paused.

'Rebecca?' asked Joy, 'anything wrong?'

'No. not really. If you don't include trying to get three boys up and out the door in the morning, cook them all a meal they will enjoy and eat and keep the house tidy after them. No aside from that life is just peachy. Except for my wardrobe woes.'

'Well I'm no Mary Poppins so I can't help you there,' said Joy smiling at her.

'That my dear is one you will have to sort on your own. So let's get to sorting out your wardrobe woes once and for all. Rebecca we'll start with you since I'm looking at you now.'

'Great, how do I make the most for less.'

'That is simple. Twelve pieces will give you enough clothes for something different every day for a bit over three months. Do you think you can do that?'

'Sounds good to me.'

'All right. You need two jackets, four bottoms, skirts, trousers or capris, your pick. Then three long or three-quarter sleeve tops and three camisoles. Now the trick here is that every piece must go with every other piece. So go home and see which jackets you have that fit. Chances are your jackets will all still work as you are losing weight from your bust, waist and hips and not your shoulders. If you want to do your jackets up you may just need to move the buttons by a centimetre. Next look at which pants and skirts you have that fit. You may find that you only need to have the waist taken in by a couple of centimetres. Any more than that and you will be looking for new pieces as they won't tailor down that small. Unless it is a straight skirt and you give it two entirely new side seams. Anything else will go out of shape. Look at your jackets and bottoms. Do your jackets go with at least two bottoms and your bottoms with at least one jacket? Sideline anything which has no partner at this point.' Rebecca was writing down everything Joy was saying and nodding intently to herself.

'Now you need to look at all of your tops. Anything that is hanging on you, get rid of now. If it doesn't look fabulous it is taking up prime real estate in your wardrobe and drawers. Since we are coming into summer you'll find this layering technique great for getting a variety of looks from only a few pieces. As long as you have a full range of camisoles you'll find they will change the look of any top and they will help cover any cleavage that may get exposed with some of the deeper neckline tops on the market now. That look may be fine for when you and Justin are going out but my guess is you don't want to be displaying all you've got when you drop the boys at school.'

'You can say that again.'

'So you'll probably find you don't need to buy that much. It is so much cheaper to go and have alterations done on clothing that is still looking good just not fitting you properly. I have always had my clothes altered as soon as I bought them. Would you believe for years I had people convinced everything I wore was tailor made due to the fit I always had. Not tailor made just tailored to fit. Big difference in price and ease.'

'Here I was thinking I'd have to get a whole new wardrobe. That is so simple. Makes me feel silly I hadn't thought of it myself.'

'But you won't forget it, will you?'

'No way. Thanks Joy.'

'Louise, you are worried about how to dress for the gallery. Is that right?'

'Oh Joy, you should see everyone coming in. They are the most eclectic bunch of people and they all look so arty and well connected and then there is little old me. How do I fit in with them?'

'The first thing you must realise that you weren't asked by Sergei to work at the gallery because he wanted you to look a certain way. Well, no that's not true. He does want you for how you look but it is how you look with your eyes and not your body.'

'That doesn't help me to dress though.'

'You have some lovely clothes now. Just as Rebecca is creating a wardrobe from a few key pieces I want you to do the same and I want you to look at what you can add in the way of accessories. Art is about how something is put together. You are put together very well but you might like to go shopping for some scarves and some wonderful pieces of jewellery art you could wear around your neck. That single piece of amber said more than wearing layers and layers of jewellery.' Cynthia made a small sniffing sound at the mention of the less is more focus as she had been one to live by the philosophy that more was never enough.

'Don't worry Cynthia we are dressing Louise right now not you.'

'Sure thing, I'll wait my turn.'

'So Louise do you think you could find a few pieces to dress yourself up with. The simpler your outfit the more expressive you can be with your jewellery and the impact you will have and I believe the more comfortable you will be in yourself. Remember you don't want to outshine the paintings you want to help people see the value and the beauty within them.'

'Well that is not so scary. Here I thought I was going to have to compete with men in cravats and women in exotic European outfits.'

'Never compete. It will be your downfall. Just be you. It is as simple as that. A tulip can never be a rose and doesn't want to be.' Louise enjoyed thinking of herself as a tulip. Simple and refined. Cynthia however was getting twitchy in her seat as she always did when she felt things were not turning to her quickly enough.

'My dear Cynthia. Whatever happened to Cyclone Cynthia? You are looking very polished and professional today.'

'So I should. I bought this outfit last week and it cost me a bomb.'

'And what does it go with in your wardrobe?'

'This, well nothing really.'

'Cynthia this is not going to work. You are going to end up with a wardrobe of clothes and nothing to wear.'

'You can say that again.'

'I want you to separate your entire wardrobe into jackets, trousers, skirts and tops. Place your play clothes in the same order in one section and the clothes which are more in keeping with your new role in another section of your wardrobe. That way when you are looking for work clothes they are all together and not messed up with your party clothes. The shoes that suit each section should live under that area of the wardrobe.'

'Have you seen how many shoes she has?' laughed Rebecca. 'She needs a separate wardrobe for those alone.'

'Now that is the pot calling the kettle black,' returned Cynthia to Rebecca. It had already been outlined that Rebecca was the shoe queen of the trio.

'I think I get the picture,' continued Joy. 'You have two options Cynthia, shoe trees for your shoes or keep them in plastic boxes so that you can see what is what or take a photo and put it on the end of each box if you have as many shoes as Rebecca. But however you do it, separate your work and play clothes. That will save you from making any more errors in what you can and cannot wear to work.'

'Can do. But how will that give me more clothes.'

'Ah that is going to be planning on your part. Once you have separated your clothes I want you to see what may or may not mix and match. Then create a list of those pieces which are loners and when you shop you must promise me this. You will only buy anything which will go with at least two other things already existing in your wardrobe. There are to be no more orphans in your wardrobe. I want the League of Nations where everything is happily working with everything else.'

'So no more outfits?'

'Not for the time being. Not one off, stand alone outfits that is. You have to get more co-ordinating and play with what you have. Otherwise you will never have any money to spare for anything you may want to do.'

The girls had hoped to remain later than usual today but Cynthia had to go back to the office to prepare for a client she was meeting with the next day. Rebecca got a call from the school and had to pick up Luke who had got hit by a football during sports and had a nasty headache and Louise wanted to go back to the gallery even though it was her day off.

Joy cleared up their cups humming to herself. She knew the girls were going to be okay from here on in.

Chapter 15.

The finishing touch

The finishing touch

A year had passed since the girls had last been to Joy's for coffee. Louise had very little spare time on the weekends as Sergei's gallery was receiving rave reviews from all corners of the globe and every six weeks there would be a new and upcoming artist they would be launching. She had dived into the world of modern art. Preparing the collections. Overseeing the hanging of the artwork. The placement around the gallery so that the right light was hitting each piece and the story that they told individually flowed to give an overall mood to the collection. This next collection was going to be extra special to her. This next collection would include a couple of her own paintings. She was painting under her maiden name as she didn't want to be confused with Jeffrey Smart. Not that that would be a bad thing. The man was a genius but she wanted her own identity and didn't want to be constantly asked if they were related.

Sergei had seen promise in her eyes and knew he was right when he had seen some of Louise's work. He could see talent even when there was no paint around. For the past twelve months he had been mentoring Louise to develop her painting skills. Often they would get together on a Tuesday and paint together either in his studio or occasionally if the weather was good they would go to the beach or to the mountains and paint. Louise had been working on a special piece. This landscape was worked from the dunes above the beach at Mentone. It was filled with her hopes as a young girl and her anguish from the night she went there when she realised that her life with Rob was over for good. People commented on how much emotion was in the painting and she had had many offers to buy her painting. This one would never be for sale. That much she knew for sure. Louise had sent an invitation to the girls to attend her opening. Well it was not exactly her opening as she was sharing the walls with three other talented artists that Sergei had discovered but to the entire world it felt as if it was hers alone. She couldn't wait to see the girls and catch up. They were going to have dinner afterwards to catch up and to celebrate. There was so much to celebrate she thought to herself as she looked at the invitation in her hand.

Rebecca was so excited as she was preparing herself for the evening with the girls at the gallery. Her mind drifted back to the anguish she had felt getting ready for the school reunion. Wow, that was nearly two years ago now. How much had changed. She had dropped two dress sizes and was now working four days a week, from 10am to 3pm. She hadn't taken up the offer of a promotion with her own promotional work as she still wanted to be available for the boys when they got home from school. She was busy enough as it was. Rebecca couldn't believe how well she was doing with her work though. Only last month she had been awarded a prize for being demonstrator of the month and reaching her sales goals. Her prize had been a new mini microwave. This one would cook and crisp finger food so the boys could come home from school and she would have some frozen sausage rolls ready for them in half the time it took in the oven.

Tonight Rebecca had decided upon recreating a look inspired by Betty Paige. It was what she called an adult night out so she didn't mind dressing up and glamourising herself. As opposed to the kid's nights where she dressed nicely but in a manner more befitting a mum rather than a yummy mummy. She had curled her dark hair into long ringlets and wore a navy 1950s inspired silk dress with a small net underskirt. Her jewellery was silver with tiny red hearts. She had her red lipstick on and had painted extended eyeliner along her upper lids to extend her eyes. She had bought herself a new pair of peep toe red shoes as well. In her hand she had a small clutch to complete the picture.

She was looking at the invitation which had arrived in the mail today and couldn't believe how far the three girls had come together. This was just another page in the marvellous book of their life.

The night of the exhibition was a huge success and Louise couldn't believe that both of her paintings had red spots on them by the end of the evening to mark them sold. She was so disappointed that Cynthia wasn't able to make the opening but she knew they would all be catching up afterwards. She had been interstate visiting a client and had to catch a plane back which didn't get her into Melbourne in time for the opening. She had promised Louise that she would pop in over the weekend and have a good look at everything.

'So where did you book?' Rebecca asked Louise.

'Café Club.'

'Where?'

'Joy's.'

'Oh that's fantastic. I hear she has a great tapas menu now and it would be so great to see her. I am surprised she wasn't here tonight,' said Rebecca as she slid her arms into her cropped jacket which showed her newly narrowed waist off to its best advantage.

'Joy was meant to be here but Toby, her night manager was sick so she had to cancel at the last moment. Anyway if she was here she wouldn't have been in the café tonight so that is a double bonus. She said she'll slide away from behind the bar to come and chat to us.'

'You still see a bit of her then?' asked Rebecca.

'Yeah, I think there is something more than friendship between her and Sergei but don't say anything, they both are very private but I am sure that the nude hanging in his office was Joy. But you can only see her from behind so I am only guessing.'

'So do you think Joy and Sergei were, you know, when William was alive?'

'Oh God no. Joy play up on William. No chance. Though I think in Joy's modelling days she was a model for Sergei and I think that is how they met. I feel he has been in love with her for a very long time though.'

'So what did you think of the invitation?'

'Absolutely blew my mind it did. What about you.'

'Same. As soon as I saw it I started crying. Look, speak of the devil, there's Cynthia.'

'CYNTHIA, we're over here.'

Rebecca in all of her glamour, forgot herself and ran over to her friend and threw her arms around her.

'Congratulations, I am so happy for you. Show me the ring!' Cynthia who could never be called coy lifted her left hand to display one of the largest engagement rings that the girls had ever seen.

'Holy cow is that two carats?'

'Two point five but who is counting?' Cynthia held her hand out so that she could admire it even more. It still amazed her that not only was Mike the greatest man she had ever met he was loaded as well.

It had turned out that Mike had a reason to keep Cynthia at a distance. Aside from the fact that he was in the middle of juggling his brother's work in America and establishing a new office here in Australia. The Cere's and Croft Financial Advisors were a global institution that were exceptionally well known in Europe, North America and Asia. Yet they were not so big here in Australia. When he had run into Cynthia the first time he had only just arrived in Melbourne and had to run away to make some calls to the office in America. Hence he was working through the night whilst trying to start up an office here in Melbourne. The time they had run into each other in her office he was looking for staff instead of looking for work but he was tired of girls throwing themselves at his money. He thought he would see if this firecracker who took his breath away was the real deal or another gold digger. He made her boss promise not to tell her anything about him and as there were privacy clauses around all clients' information, Cynthia didn't imagine there was any more she could find out about him that he hadn't told her. Those first few months poor Mike was working day and night but now that the Melbourne office was established and his brother was back running the American office he had evenings free to properly get to know Cynthia. Very quickly they had discovered that they were ideal for each other and Cynthia had settled into a life less hectic than she had known in years. She had found where she was meant to be.

They clattered into the café and Joy had their special table down in the back corner ready for them. It was Rebecca who noticed the seating and called out to Joy.

'I think we are one short Joy, there are only five chairs and there are six of us.' Joy swung around and was about to respond when Louise stepped in.

'I only booked for five.' At that point Rebecca noticed that Tom who had been at the gallery had not followed them to dinner.

'Sit down I've got lots to tell you.' The girls sat together as Justin and Mike went to the bar to have a drink and give the girls ten minutes to catch up. They knew there was no point getting in on this conversation.

'Come on Mike, let me buy you a beer. Those girls are just going to be talking about men and wedding dresses for the next half an hour.

They won't even notice that we are missing.' Rebecca and Cynthia smiled at their men as they walked away and resumed their usual positions to catch up. Even Joy managed to move herself down to their end of the bar to *do some paperwork.*

'Joy come and join us, you know this story as much as anyone.' With that Joy put down her pen and sidled into Mike's seat next to Cynthia.

'So where's Tom?' asked Cynthia. I was looking forward to seeing him. Cynthia's usual impish grin followed any mention of Tom. Anyone who knew her better would have thought that she had the hots for him, and not Mike.

'I called it off with Tom.'

'You what. Don't tell me he was playing around on you too?'

'Cyn, not everyone plays around on me. Speaking of players Rob has split up with the masseur.'

'No?' echoed Rebecca and Cynthia.

'So does that mean you guys are getting back together?' asked Rebecca.

'No. He's tried. But our marriage breakdown took two to destroy it and it will take two to repair it and I don't want to. I loved Rob, but as a mate and father to our children. We've finished raising our kids, it's time for me to focus on myself. I'm not sure how that will be but that is all that I know so far.'

'But what happened with Tom. I thought you guys were getting along really well. And he was so dishy.'

'Stop it Cyn. Tom was great. Is great. He came along tonight but we are not suited. He does the football thing. The mate's thing. The weekends away with all of his friends. He is always with all of his friends. Don't get me wrong he is an amazing man and if I was more social I would love it but I love my time on my own. I love the fact that I am painting now. I love my life on my own.' The four women sat back in companionable silence. Thinking through all that they had lived through and shared with each other over their time together in the corner of the café here with Joy.

'Did you get my invite Joy?' asked Cynthia.

'Yes I did, thank you.'

'So you'll be coming to our engagement party?'

'Yes I will, but have you thought this through Cynthia?' The girls were surprised that such a question would come from Joy's mouth. The woman who had encouraged them, pushed them when they were too scared to move forward and held their hand as they did.

'Yes, of course I have. What do you mean by that comment?'

'Well my dear, have you realised that as soon as you are married you can no longer lay claim to being Cynful but you will now be Cyncere.' The girls erupted into gales of laughter as tears started running down their faces. They all came in close and hugged each other. When the noise they were making reached the boys at the bar they thought they had better get back to their women and settle the situation down or they may get kicked out. When they saw Joy in amongst it all they weren't too sure what to do but decided too much fun was being had that they were missing out on.

Once the boys returned Joy congratulated Mike and moved aside for him to take his seat with his fiancé. She then returned to work. It was a busy night and she knew she was going to miss the girls but this was not the end of their story but the beginning. To give them some privacy she moved to the other end of the bar. There on the table in the opposite corner were three couples. They were a mixed bunch who had the comfortable appearance of all knowing each other well. Yet something was missing. Somehow the atmosphere at their table was missing the zest and spontaneity of the other corner. There was a pall hanging over the group.

'I wonder ...' she thought and she heard William in the back of her mind.

'Joybell, you can't fix everyone's problem.'

'Oh yes I can,' she said aloud as she made her way over to the other table.

Chapter B1.

Goal setting –
Set your goals and set yourself free

Goal setting –
Set your goals and set yourself free

Goals are the foundation for success. If you know where you are going you will know when you have arrived. I could go on and on here with wonderful little sayings about setting and achieving goals but the bottom line is:

If you don't have a plan, how will you celebrate getting there?

Setting and having goals are vital to reaching your potential, achieving what you desire and living an accomplished life. You do not have to scale Mt Everest to feel accomplished. Simple things like:

1. Your family is well taken care of
2. You have filed your tax return
3. Clear out that box hiding in the far corner of the spare room

There are many reasons why people fail. Here are a few to ponder:

- They fail to plan
- They are scared of success – failure is an easy option
- They have to refocus

If you fall into group one or two then this chapter is going to be a huge wake-up call for you. If you fall into the last group, it is not a bad thing; it is just a stage in the planning cycle.

Do you think NASA landed the first rocket they sent into space directly onto the moon? No. It took years of planning and attempts until they finally had the perfect formula that they expected to achieve success with. As we know the rest is history. We do not look at the hard work they put into the landing we simply celebrate the landing. They had a goal in mind and they monumentally succeeded.

Do you think Jimmy Choo was the huge success he is from his first shoe? No, but he planned to be successful at making shoes and he was. He didn't plan to be successful at cooking. One of the most amusing sayings I have heard is hearing a person declared an overnight success. More often than not many hours, days and years have gone into that one night. Taking the time to plan what you want to achieve, outlining how your life will look and feeling in your heart what your new life will be like are the first steps to reaching your goal.

Goals are not something you need a degree to manage. They can be as simple or as complex as you like and guess what? No one else can tell you what your goals are. Only you can and that makes you the master of your destiny.

You don't have to wait for the new moon, for the beginning of the week or the end of a month. Waiting until it is the right season or the start of a year to begin working on your goals. You can begin, right here and right now.

I hope I have got you excited now to start planning your future. Every one of us is an individual so I do not believe the process that will work for one person will work for everyone. Within this chapter are various methods of goal setting. Each has worked for me at a different stage of my life for a different purpose. Read through each of these to decide which process suits you the best. Before you do though be clear on what you want to achieve. All the planning in the world cannot help you if you don't know what you want your outcome to be. No matter how big or small your unfinished business is, plan to complete it. It is an amazing feeling to know it is completed. The personal sense of achievement is worth the time spent focusing on what you need to do. Don't procrastinate any longer. You can have whatever you want. Just plan for it.

Start with the end in mind

You cannot plan until you know where you are going.

What do you want to achieve?

What is the time frame you want to complete your task in?

How will you feel when you have completed this project/plan/goal?

With anything, knowing what you want to achieve can make the goal planning so much easier. Once you have your target in mind you can start looking at how you can reach this target. If it is to lose weight you might start looking at how diet and exercise could impact on your life. If it is to get a promotion you could start looking at what you should be doing to be deemed qualified for the promotion. Your goal may be to get your house in order. To do this you may plan to tackle a different room every day or every week depending upon your schedule or simple to employ a cleaning lady. Think about all of the options you have ahead of you to reach your goals.

Action Plan: Take a pen, piece of paper and 30 minutes for yourself. Sit in a place where you will be undisturbed and start writing down all that you want to achieve. As you write, do not just write I want to be slimmer, I want to be richer, I want a fabulous relationship. If your goal is to be slimmer, write down exactly how much you want to weigh. Then add how your clothes will fit you. Don't bother what size you will be as I will discuss this later but size is irrelevant as potentially you can find a designer who will have clothing in that size already to fit you. Add to this outline when you want to have this goal achieved by and make it realistic. You cannot expect to lose five kilograms in five minutes. Believe me though by the end of this book I can have you looking as if you lost five kilograms in five minutes. That is all to do with illusion. When you outline how much you want to lose, exactly when you want to have it gone by and how you will feel, you can then start working out how you will achieve this goal.

Three must do items per day

This is a simple way to begin this process. Our daily life can get so filled with unnecessary distractions that we start the day with our 'to do' list and find by the end of the day we haven't achieved anything. Often we can spend so much time writing our 'to do' that there is no time left 'to do' anything. I start my day with a piece of paper that I write down three things that have to be done that day. Today will include a chapter of this book but may also include post a cheque and return a phone call. I write items that I know if I do not do them today that they will only play in my head tomorrow. You may wish to write out your list of three must do's the night before you leave your desk, as you lie in bed in your journal or first thing in the morning. By writing them down you are able to record what you have achieved should you like to reflect on your achievements. If this is the case write them in a diary or journal.

Action plan: Decide if you are going to save these items (if so you will want to use a diary or journal) or toss them away as you finish them which means a note pad or the back of a piece of paper that you are finished with. This option is for the environmentally conscious who wish to minimise their use of paper. Then decide if you are going to write them first thing in the morning, before you leave your desk at night, or before you go to bed. Commit to doing this for three weeks and then see how a delicious habit is forming that clears your mind and your life.

Chunking down a big goal

Sometimes the whole process of goal setting can be too big and too impossible to believe it is possible. This process will help you make the seemingly impossible possible.

First start with the end result as you have done in the previous three tasks. The next step is to list 20 ways you could achieve this end task. Then from the list of 20 possibilities select one and list another 20 ways you could achieve this result. Keep going with all of the possibilities until you have a path and selection that is all very do-able to you.

Another option is to look at the goal as a series of steps and take it one step at a time. Give yourself smaller tasks to complete and before long you will have travelled further than you thought possible if you have kept the bigger picture in the front of you the whole time.

Take for instance losing weight. You may have five kilograms to lose. Stop focusing on the five and focus only on one kilo at a time. Rather than thinking you have to go on a huge diet, look at one small thing you could take out of your daily diet that will not be too difficult. This may be having half a teaspoon less of sugar in your coffee or switching your afternoon biscuit for a piece of fruit.

Do you see how breaking down any plan into small bite sized chunks will make it easier? Or smaller steps. Having to scale Mt Everest is a big task but having to walk 100 metres in a day is very do-able.

Action plan: Decide if the goal you have in mind will be easier to achieve if you break it into manageable chunks. Look at the steps involved to reach your goal.

Goal picture board

We all plan our future differently. If you desire a new life with a different look and feel to the life you currently have you could try creating a picture board with images of everything you want in and out of life. This is making your intent much clearer. It allows you to hold fast to your vision. You may place pictures of a better car or house, clothing you like or even vacation spots you would like to go to. Be clear on your intent. I accidentally did this when I was 18. I saw a large clock while backpacking in Rome. There was no way I was going to get it home in my backpack, nor could I afford it. So I took a photo because I thought it was so fantastic. Two months after I was home I was working at a trade show and there was the clock. The importer sold it to me for wholesale. Another example happened to my husband. He saved a photo of a motorcycle he saw for sale only to realise five years later that the bike he had just purchased was the exact bike in the photo. You can keep the pictures in your diary, your wallet or display them on a large canvas in your house. The choice is yours. Go ahead and dream. If you can dream it, chances are you can do it.

Action plan: Buy a large sheet of poster paper, find some scissors, glue and magazines. Start looking through the magazines and cut out everything that supports or represents your goal. Paste these pictures onto your board and hang or stick that board where you can see it every day. If you are very good with your computer you can find pictures from the Internet and cut and paste them onto a word document then print out those pages. These pages can get printed and put into a frame and hang them where you will see them every day.

Meditation focusing on outcome

Through all aspects of goal setting it is important to be clear on what you wish your outcome to be. A brilliant way to get clarity around what you desire is to meditate upon the desired outcome. There are many great guided meditations to help you through this process so find one that resonates with you. Set aside around 20 to 30 minutes each morning to meditate. Find yourself a comfortable space to sit, close your eyes and tune out on the world. You may find repeating a mantra or a sound will still your mind. Yes 'omm' does work. Focus on what you want, be clear here to see in your mind what you want, not what you don't want. As I said before, be very clear upon your outcome. Many years ago I used this technique somewhat successfully. I was tired of the job that I was in so I envisaged myself walking up and down stairs carrying manila folders and feeling very important. I manifested that destiny alright. I become the accounts clerk in a business that was in a two storey house. All I did was go up and down the stairs with folders in my arms. Not exactly the job that I had imagined. I think I should have included a few more tangible aspects to my imaginings. This is just as important as when you are dreaming about your perfect man. Make sure you include some personality in with his physical and financial state and while you are at it ensure he is single with no excess baggage. There is nothing worse than discovering Mr Right is Mr Right-for-someone-else.

Action plan: Find some quiet time, some music that is easy to listen to and not invasive on your thoughts, or a guided meditation. Sit quietly and allow the images that represent your goal to float into your mind. Keep adding to the picture until it looks, sounds and feels real to you. Hold fast to this image.

Do a lifestyle chart to see where you spend your time

Often we do not realise how much time that we spend in different activities in our life. We can feel incredibly busy only to discover that a lot of time is spent procrastinating and time wasting. There is an example of a lifestyle chart at the end of this chapter. Fill it in as well as you can. Have a look at where there are gaps that you could use for achieving your goals and see where you spend the rest of the time. You may have to do this chart over a whole month to get an idea of where and how you spend your time. Or you may wish to fill it out as you go through your week as you may be surprised how much time is spent doing things you were not even aware of.

Action plan: Fill in the chart either for your average week or chart your actions over a week or month to see what your lifestyle looks like.

If you are trying to lose weight it will help if you include into this chart what you eat and when. This will increase your awareness if food intake is an issue for you. Sometime snacking as you prepare the children's meals and lunches can be more dangerous than you ever realised.

List everything you have to do in the next month

In relation to the list of three daily items it can help to see what you already have on your calendar for the next month to see if you have room to assign any additional tasks or to become clearer on what has to be completed first before you start anything else. I have some girlfriends who never have time for their family as they are so busy with their friends and career that their family suffers. It is not silly to make sure you diarise time to be spent with your loved ones as you do not want them to suffer as you focus on the outcomes you wish to attain in your life.

Action plan: Either using a diary or a month to a page calendar chart write down everything that you have to do for the coming month. See where there are gaps that you can add tasks that will add to you reaching your desired goal or where there are blocks of workload that either needs to be moved or worked around.

See what can be delegated

Based on the last two points you will find your time taken up by chores or jobs that could and should be easily delegated away to others. This may be hiring the services of an ironing lady, a housecleaner or even a bookkeeper. Having a busy life is great if you do not want to feel bored with your routine but it can become all consuming if you are doing tasks that are either detrimental to your time or your skills. Learning to delegate can be a very liberating exercise.

Action plan: Look at what you do that you either do not enjoy or do not need to do. If you did not do this chore would your life be easier and if so what is that ease worth to you?

Start to say no – be assertive

Whilst you are goal setting one of your goals may need to be to learn to say no to anything that does not help you and your long term goal. This may mean saying no to extra work if you are feeling overwhelmed. It may mean saying no to that piece if chocolate in the afternoon if you are trying to lose weight or it may mean saying no to a sale item that is not ideal for you if you are trying to rebuild your image, your wardrobe or your bank balance. Frankly you should be saying no to anything in life that is not ideal, be it a shoe, a handbag or a man.

Action items for goal setting

Take some time today to list your goals and the steps you are going to take to achieve them. Write them out as if they are happening today.

Email your goals to me at Clare@claremaxfield.com.au. I will keep these safe and return them to you a year later.

	Mon	Tue	Wed	Thu	Fri	Sat	Sun
6–8 am							
8–10 am							
10–12 am							
12–2 pm							
2–4 pm							
4–6 pm							
6–8 pm							
8–10 pm							
10–12 pm							

Chapter B2.

Discover your own personality

Discover your own personality

While it is important to recognise your shape for the line and dimensions, the most important aspect of your dressing style will be your personality. You may have the identical body shape to your girlfriends but your needs and style could be completely different.

Style personalities

There are seven predominant style personalities.

For the person who is wearing clothing that suits their personality they will always be congruent and confident with their appearance. By knowing how to adjust a style to suit many different occasions this individual will separate themselves from everyone else who simply picks up what is in fashion with no regard for the finished impression.

Personality stereotyping

Style	Careers	Get the Look	Impact
Dramatic Extreme form and length Bold and large prints Dramatic accessories Highly structured	Entertainers Fashion Advertising Executives High flyers Writers Publishers	Sharp hairstyle High colour contrasts Stylised jewellery High heels Skirts above knee Bold make-up Large accessories	Authorative Creative Individual Contemporary
Creative Unconventional Any style in any combination Imaginative Mixed suits	Actors Fashion designers Interior decorators Artists Stylists	Avant-garde hairstyle Mix textures and styles Layer clothes in unusual manner	Unconventional Effusive Revolutionary Innovative
Feminine Softly structured Draping styles Small details Soft textured fabrics	Not for corporate jobs Boutique owners Cosmeticians Beauticians	Soft fluid outfits Light to medium colours Softly styled hair Court shoes with a small to high heel Slip on shoes	Vivacious Idealistic Visionary Sensitive Emotional

Classic
Tailored
  clothing
Timeless
Semi-fitted
Sensible
Rich elegent
  colours
	Finance
	Management
	Marketing
	Hotels
	  management
	Banking
	Human
	  Resources
	Lawyers
	Accountants
		Tidy appearance
		Stockings with
		  skirts
		Medium height
		  heels
		Court shoes
		2–3 colours max
		Button up shirts
		Med–Dark
		  colours
		Low to medium
		  contrast
			Respectable
			Authoritative
			Conservative
			Trustworthy
			Intellectual
			Quiet

Relaxed
Casual style
Comfortable
  fabrics
Minimal
  accessories
Casual sporty
  styles with
  little structure
Functional
	Horticulture
	Engineering
	Social services
	Child care
	Teaching
	IT
	Chiropractor
	Photographer
		Relaxed tousled
		  hair
		Open neck tops
		Layered clothing
		Low contrast
		Flat shoes
		Relaxed jacket
		Natural fibre
		  trousers
			Approachable
			Caring
			Level headed
			Practical

Refined
Quality clothing
Quality fabrics
	Corporate
	  executive level
	Retired
	Charitable
	  works
		Perfectly
		  groomed
		Designer suits
		Quality earrings
		Flawless
		  make-up
			Flawless
			Graceful
			Dignified

Sensual
Close fitting
  clothing
Overtly feminine
	Masseuse
	Dancer
	Fashion
	  co-ordinator
		Form fitting
		  clothing
		Mary Jane shoes
		  with high
		  kitten heels
			Sexy
			Voracious
			Virile

Dramatic

Dramatic general description

The Dramatic woman won't be accused of being a shrinking violet. Her presence will be visible and she won't be overlooked in the crowd. She doesn't care how tight, how short or how long anything is. As long as it makes a definite statement she will wear it. Even though it is most commonly worn by people with high contrast anyone can be dramatic by simply using the strongest colours in their palette in the highest contrast afforded them.

Dramatic hair and make-up

Her style is short and sharp, or long and restricted. She won't have a hair out of place. Her colour will be extreme and she will spend the time to ensure her image is perfect.

Her make-up will be flawless as well and she will have either strong eyes or lips.

Dramatic pieces

At work – her suits will be firm fitting, short and sharp. She will have to be careful her skirts are not considered too risqué. High collars, large collars and tight waists will all define her style.

At play – she is a designer's dream. Casually she won't be seen dead in the off the rack pieces that everyone is wearing. Her weekend wear will be designer inspired, and again it will be short and sharp fitting.

Dramatic colours

Black, white, red, cobalt blue and fuschia. Strong geometric designs more so than patterns.

Dramatic fabrics

Simple design and plain fabrics, crisp and sharp finishes. Silk dupion and crisp cotton shirtings are favoured. Leather rather than suede, vinyl for the less well off Dramatic. The Dramatic will even put up with linen in summer, mind you hers won't be crushed.

Dramatic fit

The Dramatic has cinched in waists, stand up collars, wide spread collars, short skirts, tight skirts. Anything over scale is exactly what the Dramatic is looking for.

Dramatic footwear

Towering stilettos, sharp pointed toes, high gloss patent leather and knee high boots. These women are the extremists of fashion and don't care what damage or pain their feet must go through to look fabulous.

Dramatic jewellery

Whilst they are less is more in number of pieces, more is more when it comes to size. Earrings and brooches are favoured by the Dramatic. They are more likely to have a kerchief in the pocket of their jacket or a brooch on their lapel than wear a necklace.

Their watch will be large and stylish but not chunky.

Dramatic underwear

She will be happiest in underwear that is a little bit different. She will like interesting trim on her underpants, preferring G-strings (thongs) or boyleg to the mundane panties other women wear. She will love exciting colours like black, red or leopard print. Her bras will be demi or half cups. She may even have body slimmers in her drawers to keep her looking gorgeous.

Dramatic accessories

Patent leather bags either large or slim line, never fussy. Her pen will be large and considered more suited to a man's hand for fit. Her perfume will leave a lasting impression

Creative

Creative general description

The Creative woman walks her own line. She will not to be dictated to by convention or fashion magazines. She will delight in wearing a variety of colour and styles that reflect her moods and personality. If anyone else tries to copy her they will fail miserably.

Creative hair and make-up

Her hair can range from flowing locks to a very short and dramatic look. Colour will be something she will experiment with and may have nothing to do with her personal colouring, much to my dismay. Make-up will be over the top or barely there.

Creative pieces

At work – Creatives will have trouble conforming to the corporate world. Mind you their personality will suit them to the creative fields of any kind of design. She will most probably be most comfortable wearing separates and accessorising at work with oversized scarves and wraps. Dramatic, beads, belts and bangles will complete her look. She must make sure she doesn't annoy the rest of the office jangling as she works.

At play – everyday will be something new for her and the only thing that can be predicted is that nothing will be predictable.

Creative colours

The brighter and bolder, the better for this woman. Pastel colours don't really fit into this scenario very well unless it is somethng widely exotic. Fabrics will feature strong colours, abstract and animal prints.

Creative fit

The 'creative fit' has no rhyme or reason to it. If it feels good and looks good it will work.

Creative footwear

Creatives tend more towards comfort and functionality than the latest fashion. As long as it looks interesting with her outfit she will wear it.

Creative fabrics

There is no right or wrong here. From PVC to satin, silk and everything else ever created. The world is her oyster.

Creative underwear

She will be happiest in underwear that is as fun as her personality. Bright colours, mix and match patterns. Tops and bottoms will always be different.

Creative jewellery

Large, expressive and unpredictable. Faux pieces are her favourites. Beads and baubles that glitter, to stone and wood that have a dramatic earthy and tribal effect.

Her watch will most probably be large with an elaborate patterned band.

Creative accessories

If it holds what she needs she will carry it. Her pen will be anything from a large chunky fabulously expensive Mont Blanc in orange to a brilliant coloured plastic biro.

When it comes to perfume again Her choices will be anything but ordinary.

Feminine

Feminine general description

The Feminine personality is instinctly womanly and sometimes romantic in her appearance. There is nothing masculine, sharp or hard in her finish. Feminine women will take the time to attend to the smallest detail of their outfit. They will have soft features and soft lines to their body. Scarlet O'Hara is the goddess of all Feminine women.

Feminine hair and make-up

Pretty is the only way to describe a Feminine woman. She has delicate even features. Her hair is never short. It is either a soft bob, at its shortest or a long mane of wavy hair that can be worn up in all manner of elegant or sexy styles. Feminine women will often retain their hair and make-up not just for years but decades, but be aware that she is not falling into an age trap where what was once beautiful is now tragic.

Feminine pieces

At work – the truly Feminine woman will find it demanding wearing the structured corporate wardrobe. She will be most comfortable in light coloured suits, co-ordinates with a slightly structured jacket. She will have no problem wearing the feminine court shoes.

At play – the Feminine woman will be most comfortable in her shawls and wraps for warmth. She will have a wardrobe full of comfortable dresses in a variety of lengths as well as an array of full skirts and soft blouses and knits.

Feminine colours

Think pastels, think floral and thinks bows and ribbons. Now, hopefully, not all at once. The Feminine woman enjoys softness to her colours and patterns.

Feminine fabrics

Her fabrics will welcome touch. Tactile and fluid fabrics such as silk charmeuse, satin, fine cottons such as batiste cottons, soft wools, angora and cashmere.

Feminine fit

The Feminine fit has a softly tailored finish. There are plenty of ruffles, curves and folds in her outfits. Nothing is tight; in fact everything will flow, especially as she walks.

Feminine footwear

More is not enough for her when it comes to shoes. She will have a variety of styles from flat ballet slipper styles to medium high court shoes. In a variety of colours to match every outfit and a variety of trims on them. Again most of her shoes will be leather, not too shiny and not at all chunky.

Feminine underwear

She will be happiest in underwear made from lace and silk. She will love to wear matching sets, French knickers and anything that will make her feel very sexy and feminine.

Feminine jewellery

From Grandma's cameo, to a delicate strand of fine glass beads, she will love anything delicate and feminine. Like the Classic she too will love pearls but her strand and earrings will be small and delicate. Her watch will be small with a fine band. More like a bracelet than a watch.

Feminine accessories

Her bag will be soft and unstructured to touch and look at. At work her accessories will have rounded softer edges than some of her contemporaries. Her pen could be fine gold or it may be softly coloured enamel. When it comes to fragrance her's will be delicate and maybe a little sweet

Classic

Classic general description

This woman is of medium height. She has well balanced features and is more conservative in nature. Classics often appear cautious in nature and seen as very safe. Their clothing is well maintained and will not date quickly. This woman will be cultured and concerned about her image.

Classic hair and make-up

Her hair is always well cut, nothing extreme and smartly styled. It is more often shoulder length than extremely short or long. Younger Classics will opt for a styled longer bob until they cut it into their trademark shoulder length bob. Hair may be highlighted but the colours will be safe and elegant. Highlights will be natural and well blended.

Classic pieces

At work – she will be most comfortable in a suit jacket that is teamed with a skirt or dress.

At play – on the weekends she may select casual trousers that she will team with a classic shirt and a blazer for warmth. She is not one to throw on a tracksuit for comfort. She will always have solid shoes on her feet.

Classic colours

Colours that have a medium density are the foundation of the classic wardrobe.

Business – navy, cream, taupe, warm brown and pewter
Social – navy, taupe, red and black

Classic fabrics

Plain fabrics, classic prints like houndstooth, Burberry and Prince of Wales check. Floral prints will work for her blouses in soft pastel colours. Traditional fabrics like, silks, cottons, wools and linens in a medium weight. Finer fabrics like wool crepe, fine broadcloths, silk organza and batiste cotton.

Classic fit

The Classic fit has nothing too tight or too loose. Jackets will be tapered to fit. Blouses will softly drape and skirts will be at moderate length.

Classic footwear

Classic shoes are understated. Moderate to high heels with skirts and dresses are her signature style. She will feel most comfortable in smart flat trousers shoes with her pants. Shoes will be made from leather and suede. In the evening she may select a sling black style and for comfortable daytime wear a low heeled Mary Jane or plain court shoe is more her style.

Classic underwear

The Classic will be happiest in underwear made from microfibre, which will give her a clean line at her hips and bras that do not have ornamentation that will show through her clothing. Her underwear will be in either skin tone, black or red.

Classic jewellery

Precious metals and precious and semi precious stones will be her favourites. She will love her pearls and prefer chains in gold or silver rather than imitation jewellery.

Her watch will have a plain face with either Roman numerals or plain numbers. Her band will be gold, silver or fine black leather.

Classic accessories

Leather will be important whether it is a simple handbag with a shoulder strap or an elegant lady's briefcase. She will most likely have a wardrobe full of black handbags. Her perfume will be timeless and sophisticated. Her pen will be plain gold or silver.

Relaxed

Relaxed general description

Comfort is most important to her. The idea of squeezing into restrictive clothing is not for her. She is very down to earth and matter of fact in her approach to life. The overall look of the Relaxed is less feminine without being mannish.

Relaxed hair and make-up

Less is truly more for her. If her hair is long it will be straight and worn in a no fuss manner. Shorter cuts for her will require that it will be almost a shake and go finish. Relaxed's with curl and wave are the luckiest as their hair will hold volume without the use of sprays and gels.

There is no fuss with the Relaxed make-up. In many cases the Relaxed will only wear a lip gloss and maybe some mascara. In a corporate role, she may require more make-up to give her face some depth.

Relaxed pieces

At work – suiting made out of comfortable natural fibres. Suits teemed with knits and comfortable camisoles as opposed to crisp shirts. Relaxeds will prefer a pant suit to a skirt or dress.

At play – this woman will always look as if she is either ready to work out or go walking in the country. Dresses will not feature in this wardrobe. It will be filled with comfortable trousers for winter and capris and shorts in summer. Jackets will play a major role in natural comfortable fabrics.

Relaxed colours

Everything that looks like it belongs in nature. Greens from the forest and grasses, blues from the sky and sea, browns from the trees and earth as well as sand from the dunes and the beaches.

Relaxed fit

The Relaxed fit has room to move and wears lots of layers. She would rather remove layers than freeze on her way to work. Her jackets are softly structured and skirts and trousers range from tailored to baggy.

Relaxed footwear

She will be the lady wearing her runners to work and then slipping into a pair of low suede pumps or else leaving her runners on. She will love sports shoes, lace up shoes, hiking boots and trouser shoes. Unlike many other personality dressing styles she will use her walking shoes for exactly what they were designed for, walking.

Relaxed underwear

She will be happiest in underwear made from pure cotton. She will not wear anything unnatural next to her body; she will prefer bras without under-wire if possible.

Relaxed fabrics

Fabric for her will be lovely to touch and full of texture. She will love raw silks and organic cottons.

Relaxed jewellery

Chunky and natural. Anything from nature will look good on her from small amber earrings to rough stone beads. She will not feel comfortable in anything too shiny or prissy. Her watch will be functional and most probably be held by a brown leather band.

Relaxed accessories

Backpacks, large shoulder totes and sacks are her idea of a great bag. Ideally made from hessian, brown leather or suede. Any old pen will do. Unless she has a gift which is sentimental to her. Her perfume will be fresh and organic or alternatively oriental and musky.

Refined

Refined general description

This woman is of medium height. She has well balanced features and is more conservative in nature. The Refined woman knows who she is and is seen as very elegant. Her clothing is impeccably maintained, well cut and well designed. This woman will have grace and style about her.

Refined hair and make-up

Her hair is always well cut, nothing extreme and elegantly styled. It is often shoulder length than extremely short or long. It is rare to find a young Refined. This category comes with wisdom. Hair may be highlighted but the colours will be rich and elegant. Highlights will be natural and well blended.

Refined pieces

At work – as most of her work will be charity or leading a board she will wear suits in colours as opposed to the conservative navy and blacks.

At play – her clothing if not designer will be designer inspired. She will always look immaculate and never appear slouchy, even when she is wearing casual pants on a Sunday afternoon.

Refined colours

Colours that have a medium density are the foundation of the Refined wardrobe.

Business – cream, mushroom, gunmetal grey, deep dove blue

Social – dusty pink, chocolate, gemstone colours

Refined fabrics

All natural, crisp cottons, tweeds, pure wools and silk. Generally plain fabrics over prints.

Traditional fabrics like silks, cottons, wools and linens in a medium weight. Finer fabrics like wool crepe, fine broadcloths, silk organza and batiste cotton.

Refined fit

The Refined fit has nothing too tight or too loose. Jackets will be tapered to fit. Blouses will softly drape and skirts will be at moderate length.

Refined footwear

Refined shoes are elegant. She will feel most comfortable in smart flat trousers shoes with her pants. Shoes will be made from high quality leather and suede. In the evening she may select a sling black style and for comfortable daytime wear she will still wear an elegantly tailored shoe of the highest quality.

Refined underwear

She will be happiest in underwear made from silk, which will give her a clean line at her hips, and bras that do not have ornamentation that will show through her clothing. Her underwear will be in either skin tone, black or pink.

Refined jewellery

Quality more than quantity is her motto. Precious metals and precious and semi precious stones will be her favourites. While she doesn't wear austentacious jewellery she will wear statement pieces. She will be known for her elegant earrings in gold, silver or pearl.

Her watch will have a plain face with either Roman numerals or plain numbers. Her band will be gold, silver or fine black leather.

Refined accessories

Leather will be important whether it is a simple handbag with a shoulder strap or an elegant lady's briefcase. Elegantly styled and not too chunky. Her perfume can be defined as fresh with a hint of musk.

Her pen will be fine and in gold or silver.

Sensuous

Sensuous general description

The Sensuous woman is of small to medium height. She has cherubic features and is quick to smile. She is not cheap but she cannot help but flirt. It is in her nature. She is easily hurt as she never intends to hurt or offend anyone. She has beautiful curves and loves to show them off.

Sensuous hair and make-up

Her hair is always full. She takes time with her hair and make-up. She loves to look like a woman and delights in taking care of her appearance. She would not be comfortable with short hair and will always have a full face of make-up on. Even when she is going to the gym.

Sensuous pieces

At work – in an office environment she will have trouble fitting in as the rest of the staff will constantly feel she is trying to pick up while at work. She does not mean this, it is just her nature. She will prefer skirts and dresses with little wrap tops.

At play – the weekend will find her in all her feminine glory. From floral skirts to Mary Jane shoes with bows on the toes. She may have layers of long chains around her neck or layers of pearls. She will love skin-toned fishnet tights, but worn with a pretty skirt to ensure she doesn't look cheap.

Sensuous colours

Anything pink and pretty. She will not be comfortable in black and white unless the print is small and feminine. Then she may try it. Small liberty prints, hearts and cherries will feature.

Business – mid blues, pinks and white

Social – everything feminine

Sensuous fabrics

Patterns in small print, floral, checks, seersucker. As well as fine cottons, net tulle, shantung lace, polished cottons, very fine knits, nothing chunky here.

Sensuous fit

The Sensuous fit is form fitting. This woman will wear her clothing so that it not only hugs her curves but promotes the volume and shape of her curves.

Sensuous footwear

There will be nothing sensible on her feet. Heels will be towering, if she must have a flat shoe it will be for working out only and even that may have a heel or will have pink or reflective colours on it. During the day peep toes will feature in winter and strappy sandal in summer.

Sensuous underwear

She will love pretty feminine lacey underwear. Half cup bras and frilly French style knickers. She will also have a drawer filled with shape control garments.

Sensuous jewellery

Delicate little rings will abound, small pendants will feature but so too will chunky icon pieces, large and long strands of pearls, flashy diamonds where she can afford them or their counterparts.

Time can be such a bore to her that she may not even wear a watch but if she does it will be delicate and pretty.

Sensuous accessories

She will love small clutch bags. If she is in the corporate world she will have a deep pink alligator satchel and anything encrusted with diamantes will catch her eye. Her perfume will be sweet and fruity during the day and rich and seductive at night.

When you know your personality style it can stop you from wasting time and money on clothing and accessories you feel you should have because everyone else does and then relegate these items to the back of your wardrobe, never to see the light of day. Knowing yourself and presenting yourself true to your personality will give you a clearer picture to those who meet you and there will be less chance of confusion.

Underline the words in the quiz that are most like you and see which column has the most lines in it. **Chose only one word** from each row.

If you scored mostly

As you are Dramatic
Bs you are Creative
Cs you are Feminine
Ds you are Classic
E' you are Relaxed
Fs you are Refined
Gs you are Sensual

Action items for discovering your personality

You may be a combination of two personality types.

Read through the personality outlines and see if your answer equals what is written in the description.

If you do not agree with the personality described ask a close friend. You may be hiding behind someone else's style and that is nothing to be worried about. Often when we admire someone we want a little of what they have so we try to emulate them. In this case I want you to discover who you are. You can wear a little of your hero's perfume if that helps.

A	B	C	D	E	F	G
Assertive	Adventurous	Calm	Conscientious	Approachable	Tasteful	Sensual
Charismatic	Avant-garde	Caring	Conservative	Cheerful	Serene	Cheeky
Convincing	Creative	Considerate	Efficient	Easygoing	Effortless	Tactile
Demanding	Imaginative	Endearing	Mature	Energetic	Agreeable	Surprising
Direct	Independent	Gentle	Organised	Enthusiastic	Charming	Enticing
Impactful	Innovative	Non-threatening	Reliable	Natural	Stately	Lively
Impatient	Original	Sensitive	Responsible	Straightforward	Modest	Racy
Intense	Spontaneous	Understanding	Sensible	Uncomplicated	Benevolent	Flirtatious
Self-assured	Unconventional	Warm	Trustworthy	Unpretentious	Amiable	Risqué

Chapter B3.

What's your shape?

What's your shape?

The human body will vary from person to person, but I have always hated referring to a woman's body as if she was a piece of fruit. Women's bodies are beautiful and as such should be celebrated. It is for that reason that I have likened their body to the beautiful glassware that you can find about.

Body shapes

There are six main body shapes for you to discover your own shape from. Remember we are often elements of a lot of shapes so if you cannot decide what shape you are then ask a girlfriend. You can also use soap to draw your outline on a full length mirror.

> The Cocktail glass
> The Champagne glass
> The Martini glass
> The Margarita glass
> The White Wine glass
> The luscious full bodied Red Wine glass

With all of these body shapes there will be variations that are finer and fuller than each other. Do not be surprised that just because you are a plus size that you are not automatically a ruby red wine. You may just as easily be a champagne or cocktail glass. Once you have ascertained your body shape read through the following descriptions to get an idea what will suit you best.

Which shape are you?

The Cocktail Glass – This woman has curves. Her bust and hips are close in size with a much smaller waist. There are two versions here with the cocktail glass. The long waisted woman has a defined waist and the gap from the bottom of her ribs to her hip bone is greater than 6 centimetres. The woman who has a short waist or has a difference of less than 6 centimetres from hip to ribs is referred to as a Figure 8 woman. Whilst she technically has a waist there is too small a gap for clothing to fall properly into her waist so she appears to have a straighter line to her body. The Figure 8 woman should dress more like the champagne. The champagne shape is mostly found in females when their hips and bust are the same size and their waist is, ideally on the perfect body, 25 cm (10 inches) less.

The Champagne Glass – This woman is a person who has little or no waist definition. Often their lack of having a defined waist is not as important to them as the fact that they generally have a very small bust line.

The Martini Glass – This shape is distinctively a swimmer's body. This person has broad shoulders and a narrow waist and hips. This woman's hips will be noticeably smaller than the width of your shoulders or bust.

The Margarita Glass – This woman has a full bust with a small waist and small hips.

The White Wine Glass – This person has a small bust and waist with larger hips. Your hips will be wider than your shoulders in silhouette.

The Red Wine Glass – This woman has the softest geometric shape of all. They will have a defined stomach and will endeavour to present themselves in a way so as to minimise their stomach and accentuate their shoulders.

The Cocktail Glass

You will be suited to most styles of clothing as this is considered the ideal shape and many other shapes contour their designs to give the illusion of the cocktail glass. The main consideration for the business woman with a cocktail glass figure is to retain a level of professionalism in your attire as your figure is naturally feminine and often sexy. In work clothes you should steer clear of especially feminine shapes as this will enhance your figure. Socially these clothes and fabrics will look wonderful on you.

Sleeves: You can wear all styles of sleeve except be careful of the batwing as it can make your waist appear thicker than it is

Dresses: Due to your small waist you will look great in wrap dresses and dresses that come in at the natural waist as well as Princess line seams and anything that is tapered in at the waist. Empire line dresses do not suit your body type.

Waistlines: Due to your small waist you will often require trousers and skirts to be taken in at the waist.

Great looks: For you anything that defines your waist and keeps attention up to your face.

Avoid: Be wary of straight through garments that will hide your waist. Boxy jackets and shapeless shift dresses are not your friends.

Lines: When looking at clothes the most important thing to remember is that your body is going to look its best in clothing made up of lines that softly curve.

Famous Cocktail Glass women – Catherine Zeta Jones, Drew Barrymore

The Champagne Glass

Ladies who are a Champagne Glass may want to create a waist for themselves. This can be achieved by wearing different colours top and bottom. You will look wonderful in two piece outfits with a slight tapering in your jackets to give attention to the waist.

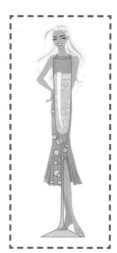

Horizontal lines in tops and scarves will visually broaden your shoulders. You will suit jackets that are very straight or with a slight tapering at the waist.

Sleeves: Look best if they are straight and crisp.

Dresses: Shirtmaker dresses and Empire line dresses are ideal. You will also suit the sheath, flapper styles and anything else that goes straight through the waistline.

Waistlines: Belts will accentuate your waist. You can wear both small and large belts either above or below the waist, it will make no difference. Minimal gathering will be required and the ideal lines are flat darts and pressed pleats.

Great looks: For you think Chanel style jackets and suits, simple lines and straight cuts.

Avoid: Do not wear anything that is excessively shaped at the waist or designed to be filled out with a fuller figure. It won't sit right on you.

Lines: You are going to look best in garments made up of and featuring straight lines.

Famous Champagne Glass women – Paris Hilton, Kate Hudson, Cameron Diaz

The Martini Glass

If this is your shape you may want to soften your shoulder line. Single breasted jackets are ideal as a double breasted jacket may give you difficulty in finding one to fit both your shoulders and your waist equally. You may prefer to wear lapels that point away from the shoulder to bring the attention down.

Wide leg pants and A-line skirts will balance out your body type. With your smaller waist you will suit shorter jackets and outfits that accentuate your smaller waist and hips. You look good in all styles of pants and can even go as far as tucking tops and jumpers in if you desire that look.

Sleeves: You will suit set-in, sharp and crisp lines. Open shoulders will look great on you and raglan sleeves will soften your shoulder line.

Dresses: Due to your larger shoulders you may find it difficult to find dresses that fit. You will look great in sleeveless, halter neck and strappy dresses.

Waistlines: You have a small waist so you should try to accentuate it where you can. This will ensure you do not appear heavier by keeping it concealed.

Great looks: Simple jackets, straight skirts with kick pleats and trim or decoration on clothing below the waist.

Avoid: You need to avoid anything that hides your small waist. Fitted dresses or suits as you will be much more comfortable in separates.

Lines: The Martini Glass shaped woman will look great in clothing that has sharper lines to it especially if you have a fine frame. If you have a muscular frame then you will suit straight and slightly curved lines.

Famous Martini Glass women – Princess Stephanie of Monaco any professional swimmers

The Margarita Glass

Often you will want to de-emphasis your bust and place more proportion into your overall body shape. While some women will cosmetically enhance their body to create this effect the natural margarita woman will be looking for solutions.

The best solutions here are soft, curved lines over the bust with sharper lines from the waist down. Short jackets will be more suitable than longer line jackets. Wraps, scarves and ponchos work well for you. When you do wear a jacket it needs to have shawl or curved lapels that point away from the bust line.

Skirts: A-line skirts, shorts and culottes can create some balance.

Necklines: A high neckline will create added emphasis to your bust so lower necklines and v-necklines can help.

Sleeves: Short sleeves level with the bust will simply create a focal line to the bust so should be avoided when minimisation is required.

Dresses: The cross over dress will look amazing on you. Other options to try are the shirt maker and coat dress, a Princess seam will allow for shape in the bust and taper the dress through your body.

Waistlines: With your small waist and hips it will mean that you often cannot buy off the rack suits. Look for separates and keep the line here simple.

Great looks: Soft tops with crisp trousers or skirts with angled sharp lines below the waist.

Avoid: Your disaster look is a jacket worn buttoned up to below your hips.

Famous Margarita Glass women – Dolly Parton, Jordan

White Wine Glass

Sometimes this shape is also referred to as the pear but I believe women should never be referred to as pieces of fruit. No matter how juicy and gorgeous they may appear, unless of course they are under five years old and as pretty as a peach. This woman will want to draw attention away from the hips and create a greater influence at the shoulders.

Shoulder pads are essential to balance out this shape. Slim line skirts and pants will look best under jackets. Your pants may need to be fuller at the waist to go over your hips so you should try and get them taken in where possible to minimise the amount of fabric built into the waist.

Sleeves: Shoulder design is important for you to appear broader in the shoulders. Puffed and pleated sleeves will work wonders. Avoid full cuffs on your sleeves as they will create a focal point to your hips.

Dresses: Dresses and jackets with peaked and pointed lapels up to the shoulders will keep the eyes focused away from the hips.

Waistlines: Ensure clothes fit your hips first and then adjust the waist to fit second. Keep gathering to a minimum so that the waist will not appear thick.

Great looks: You can play up your shoulders with scarves, brooches and collars. Select clothing that is lighter on the top and darker on the bottom.

Avoid: Skirts with too much gathering in them as they will fill your hips out. Vertical lines on the top and horizontal lines on your bottom half. Also be aware of wearing anything that stops at the widest part of your body as it will immediately draw the attention to that line and spot.

Lines: You will suit clothing that is made up of soft curved lines.

Famous White Wine Glass women – Beyonce, Jennifer Lopez

The Red Wine Glass

You will want to avoid emphasising your middle and opt for lines that flow through the body, such as jackets, long jumpers, smocks and long vests.

Your best look is clothing that is slightly shaped but overall it is unstructured. You will look best in simple designs and lines. An abundance of colour and print may make you appear larger than you are.

You can afford to bring attention to your shoulders and neckline as well.

Trousers will suit you best if they do not have pleats and have darts instead. Harsh lines and points in jackets on you will look out of place.

Soft layers of clothing camouflage this figure beautifully.

Sleeves: Sleeves need to have all decoration up at the shoulders. Wrists need to be simple to take attention away from the hips. Shoulder pads will define shoulders.

Dresses: Dresses and jackets need to fall from the shoulders in simple lines that are lightly folded or draping. Dresses and skirts cut on the bias are a great option.

Waistlines: Easing with soft gathers and pleats will soften this line.

Great looks: Over blouses, sweater and jackets with flowing skirts. Think soft lines and soft finishes. Longer lines and dropped waists.

Avoid: You must avoid anything that will focus on the waist or is too sharp. Heavy clothing will make you appear bulky.

Famous Red Wine Glass women – Queen Latifah, Maggie Tabberer

Action items

Stand in font of a mirror and decide which shape you are.

If you cannot decide which shape you are do this with a friend.

Discover if your wardrobe is supporting your body shape or hiding the beauty you truly are.

Chapter B4.

Define your assets

Define your assets

An asset by definition alone is somebody or something that is useful and contributes to the success of something. As humans we want to look the best we can and to do this it is easiest when we have people focusing on the parts of our body that we consider an asset and not our liabilities. In some instances though we spend too much time focusing on our flaws and not our fabulousness. It is 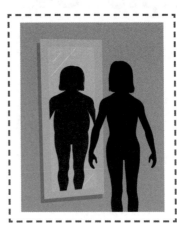 for this reason that everything about you is an asset, only occasionally we have to work with the theory of the hidden asset. Everything with our bodies is relative to what we know and where we've been.

When dressing and adorning your body it is important to see where you are placing the focus. Sometimes you have to look at yourself as removed from the situation to see what you are really highlighting. Have you ever seen a photo of yourself at a wedding or party and wondered what the heck was I thinking when I got dressed that day? We are both our worst critic and blind often to what we really look like. It is emotional blindness. There is the woman who has lost weight and cannot see yourself for who she really is and what shape she really is. There is also the other woman who cannot see how she has changed over the years and is still dressing as she did as a teenager well into her forties. When we are in our twenties, cleavage and legs look firm and great. They are our fabulous bits. When we hit our forties, the knees can start to sag, the décolletage can freckle and the skin can lose its elasticity and the full breasts you had twenty years ago have morphed into ski slopes. It's time to re-evaluate how you dress and what to turn the spotlight on and what to move into the shadows.

If you feel any of the following are one of your fabulous assets or potentially an area you would like to hide then read through the headings and see what clothing will and won't work for that asset.

Short neck – You want to create the illusion of a longer neck. This is best achieved by keeping your neck visible, wear longer necklaces, lower necklines and collars that point away from the neck. You must avoid, high collars, turned up collars, short necklaces, turtleneck tops and ruffled collars.

Long neck – In particular to shorten a neck the best steps to take are to wear high collars, mandarin collars and choker necklaces.

Relaxed shoulders – Your aim is to create a firmer line at your shoulders without using shoulder pads. Some people don't see relaxed shoulders as a problem; in fact they enjoy the softer line that they create. Strong shoulders though can offset wider hips and thighs and give a person more presence in a room. This is best achieved by shoulder pads so it is no wonder those women on *Dynasty* wielded so much power. Today, however, we can be a bit more subtle. To create a stronger shoulder line wear upward pointing lapels and jackets with decoration on the shoulders. Avoid wearing raglan or batwing sleeves, halter necklines or anything that is off the shoulder.

Big upper arms – Your aim is to slenderise the upper portion of your arms. This is an interesting part of the body. Women who have heavy upper arms are going to want to create the illusion of a slimmer arm. While those people who work out regularly will want to show off their arms. To create the appearance of a slimmer upper arm, wear ¾ sleeves and avoid any short sleeves or sleeveless Empire line dresses (these will create a focal line across to your upper arm). Remember breast pockets on jackets will also bring attention to your arms.

Busts and bellies

Bust and bellies are a constant source of conversation and women feel they either have too much or not enough. The Dramatic and the Sensual woman will focus on whether they have a large enough bust and a small enough belly. The Creative style woman really won't care. The Feminine woman will be happiest with a B or C cup. The Classic and Elegant woman will gently want to downplay her bust and the

Relaxed woman will always find it easier if they have no bust because they will not enjoy wearing the foundation garments required to keep the bust in check.

When dressing bellies and bosoms keep an eye out for where your focal points are. Buttons and pockets draw the line to exactly where they are placed. So if you are trying to minimise or hide something never put a button or a pocket on top of it.

Jacket openings can have a huge impact on the line of the body. Full busts need to be moulded into the jacket, therefore a single button jacket will always suit a full bust best. Whereas a full belly is best suited to either a jacket left open to create a central slimming core or a multi button jacket that will button over all of this area and keep it looking flat.

To minimise any pulling and exposure from shirts or jackets, which can make either a bust or a belly appear larger than it is, make sure that there is a button centred over the fullest point of the bust or stomach region. This is especially important for jackets. A jacket button that does up just above where the stomach is at its fullest can make the stomach protrude further.

Busts – The aim here is to magnify or diminish. One girl's mountain is another girl's molehill.

The art of magnifying any bust is done by wearing very high or very low cut tops. Jewellery at bust length, shorter sleeves that finish level with the bust line, Empire line tops and dresses, puffed or capped sleeves and a square or strapless neckline.

To diminish a fuller bust work with v-necklines, cross over tops, Princess seam garments, minimiser bras, short necklaces and longer sleeves. When it comes to swimwear a woman with a very full bust may be more comfortable in a top with shoulder straps as opposed to a halter top as the weight of her bust hanging around her neck can cause a headache.

Flattening a stomach – Stomachs go up and down like the changing tides. Meals, hormones and fluid: all can affect the apparent flatness or fullness of your stomach. To counteract the rising tide of tummies follow the following steps.

Avoid tight belts over your belly. Wear trousers that fit you at the waist and skirts that have flat panels as opposed to gathered or pleated waists. To create the illusion of a flatter stomach column dressing can work. This is when you wear a top and bottom in the same colour with another colour in your jacket and your jacket worn open. Avoid wearing different colours for tops and bottoms as they will bring focus to your waist and accentuate that area. Dresses are great at hiding and slimming a fuller stomach as long as they do not have a waist seam.

Full bottom – Your aim is to minimise the apparent size of your bottom from either a sway back or healthy gluteus. Clothing that falls straight down from your buttocks and those that stop just above will be your best assets. Avoid any tops stopping at the fullest part of your buttocks. Full skirts are a great concealer.

Flat bottoms – These are just as annoying as full bottoms. Women who have no bottom complain bitterly how their clothing falls flat down behind them. This is an easy fix. Fuller skirts, jackets with a peplum and well fitting clothes are better than a saggy empty bottom. Belting tops can give the appearance of a fuller bottom. Proper alterations will show this asset off to its best advantage. Remove extra folds of surplus fabric to garments.

Large hips – Women everywhere hate their hips, unless they are a screen goddess like Sophia Loren or Gina Lollabrigida whose hips are fabulous. For those of you who are too young to know these beauties go ahead and Google them. If you feel your hips are too large you will want to make them visually melt away. Your aim is to bring the focus away from your hips and add balance to your body.

To achieve this, wear correct fitting trousers even if this means buying pants that fit your hips and have them taken in at the waist. Avoid skinny jeans and wear flared or boot cut jeans. Wide collars will bring the eye up higher as will fabulous necklaces. Be wary of large bangles as they can create a focal line from the bangle across your hips just as a handbag hanging over your shoulder and swinging against your hips can do the same. Darker colours on the bottom half of your body will make that area look smaller. So leave the white skinny jeans to the girls with thinner thighs. So you want to wear white jeans I hear and you have larger thighs then wear a great pair of heels and lots of colour near your neck. It can be done.

Full calves/strong ankles – Your main concern is to attract attention away from your calves or ankles.

To do this wear plain shoes, low vamps (that means the part that covers your toes is low and doesn't go up your foot), and medium-high shaped heels. Sheer, dark hosiery will create more shape. Boots are great if you can get your legs into them. Obviously trousers are the safest bet but there is no reason you cannot wear skirts if you keep your shoes to the right size and balance for your legs.

Avoid – Short boots, strappy shoes, thick or very thin heels.

Action items

Decide which parts of your body are your best assets and decide how to highlight them.

Have a look at what other people are wearing and see where they are placing their focus.

Discuss it with your friends because what you think everyone notices may not be the case at all.

Chapter B5.

Stand out from the crowd

Stand out from the crowd

You too can stand out from the crowd for all of the right reasons. Being aware of how you appear and sound to others will allow you to be more aware of the impact you are making on others. This is my Red Riding Hood of chapters. Under each heading there is an issue with giving too little and a problem with giving too much. It is about finding the balance and being just right.

Take the time to read through these pointers to enable that light to shine on you at all times.

Stop being invisible – Women have a tendency to sit neatly, with their legs crossed and their hands folded in their laps. They take up as little space as possible. Have you noticed how men sprawl and take up space? Space assumes power. I am not recommending you sit spread eagled like a gorilla but standing with your arms slightly out or even sitting with your elbows out from your body a little can give the impression you are comfortable and confident, not a scared little mouse.

Space – There is such a thing as personal space and invading someone's space can be as invasive as breaking into their space. Depending on where you live, space is relative to the environment you live in. You will find people who live in rural communities will keep a lot of distance between them when they talk and interact. The people who live in cramped and confined living conditions will be comfortable in a very close proximity to each other. People who are tactile will often require less personal space than those who aren't. A rule of thumb though is 30 centimetres for a close conversation, 60 centimetres for a private conversation and 1 metre for a social conversation that anyone can join into. If you find people are holding their body away from you as you speak you are probably too close, so take a half step away to make them more comfortable. The other option is you need a breath mint/body spray.

Handshake – Handshakes are the way to see into what a person is really like. The number of business women who have a weak handshake amazes me. The rule of thumb here is to close your hand over the other hand and press closed. Do not squeeze – that is more of a male aggressor kind of thing to do. If the woman's hand you are shaking is soft then it is not necessary to be too firm. Do not shake with your finger tips. That is reserved for people who think they are precious and princess like. You should have stopped being a princess when you left primary school. If you encounter a man with a very firm grip, unless he is from the bush and not aware of the strength in his hand, he is most likely disrespectful to women. He is just trying to put the little lady in her place and he in all likelihood does it to men as well. Mentally you will know where to put him.

Voice – A girly sing song voice may be sweet at school but can be challenging if you want to hold authority. Listen to yourself and you will find if you want to have impact with your speech slowing down the way you speak will create a level of awareness in others as they are waiting to hear what you have to say and it will put more impact into your words. Speaking too fast will cause people to shut down and to only listen to every other word, which can cause others to get the wrong message. Finally, speaking in a very high pitch can also shut down the listener. If you are in a position where you are sharing information with an other, either consulting, instructing or even selling then a high pitch voice can be detrimental to your success. Work with a voice coach or start practising a more modulated tone.

Words – How you phrase a sentence can give you authority or take it away from you. I just sort of, kind of, had a little idea for us to think about possibly doing. Is a very lame way of saying we need to or have to do this? You have to be careful not to swing the end of your sentences with an upwards note as you can turn a perfectly sensible statement into a question.

Women are the worst offenders at softening the way they speak. Drop all of the superficial words from what you are saying and stick to the facts and what has to be said. Less words make a mightier statement.

Eye contact – This will be dependant again at whom you are speaking to as differing cultures have comfort with differing levels of eye contact. When speaking to the average Anglo Saxon person one on one then stick with the 80/20 principal. Maintain eye contact with the person with whom you are holding a conversation for 80% of the time you are speaking. Any less and you will appear unsure and lacking confidence or even shifty. Any more than that and your partner will feel they are being interrogated. When you are speaking with a group of people move your eye contact around so that you are including everyone. If you are nervous and speaking to a group I have heard it said to look over their heads at the back of the room but unfortunately you may have your audience wondering what is going on at the back. Skim their heads and look but don't focus on anyone. That can help.

Posture – Cynthia had posture appear in the chart she found in chapter three. When you are nervous you can fidget. If you find you are fidgeting, put down any tools to help like pens, rubber bands or pony tails. Sit on your hands if you must and if you are a leg tapper then sit with your two feet planted flat onto the floor. Don't slouch. Many women who were taller than their friends often find they slouch as they get older and I have noticed many women and men who work on computers develop  a habit of walking with their head forward a bit like ET. Standing up straight will not only make you appear more confident it is great for your physical wellbeing also. Your internal organs will love you and you won't suffer from back problems. Best of all standing up straight makes you look younger and slimmer. Now that's a win-win situation.

Head tilts – Head tilts are the domain of the femme fatale and can be disastrous in formal settings. When you tilt your head back you are revealing your carotid artery, which is making you appear very helpless. Watch women in sexual poses as they often employ this angle. If you use this ploy you are using your sexuality to get what you want. The opposite tilt was made most famous by Princess Diana. The head tilt down and looking up through your lashes. This is used by young girls all the time

when they are trying to get away with something. Again this is not a pose to use if you want to be taken seriously. By all means use it on your husband if he wants to know if they are new shoes you are wearing and you are trying to change the subject. Holding your head up straight with your chin tucked in a little will give you confidence without appearing cocky.

Speech – Here is where I can highly recommend the power of the pause. When you have something to say do not rush it all out at once. Listen to what is being said, and by pausing you give yourself a chance to consider your answer and the pause also allows for you to appear to be in deep thought and consideration for a well thought out response. Even if you have no idea what is going on. Rushing in with an answer can often be just filling space and sometimes the filling does not exactly fit the question.

Action items for presence:

Practise holding your body straight and your head straight.
When you talk listen for the little filling words to come out and remove them from your conversation and your written word.
Shake hands with a friend and ask them if your handshake is weak, firm or overbearing.

Chapter B6.

Colour your world

Colour your world

The girls were all put through their colour paces by Joy. Individual colour consulting is impossible unless you are face to face with the person and the colour. Understanding how colour affects you and recognising your own colour contrast though is very easy.

Contrast levels

By using this grey scale you can take a photograph of yourself and see how your hair skin and eyes contrast with each other to create your own contrast levels. If you find it hard to discern which colours suit you against the grey scale then print any photo up in black and white and it will make it much easier. Another way to work it is to look at the colours through a piece of red Perspex.

Have a look at the two women on these pages and see how both have similar medium level of contrast yet the first face is medium low and the second face is medium to high.

This girl has hair at level 5, her skin is at level 2 and her eyes are at level 4.

This means the greatest difference between her hair skin and eyes will rate at 3. With her skin rating at 2 and her hair rating at 5.

This woman will always look better in clothing and accessories that have a low to medium level of contrast. If she wears a skin tone top she should wear jewellery in the same tones as her hair or eyes to create the perfect level of harmony. Should she wear something bold and deep the impact will be more about the garment or the accessory than her.

Notice how when we add colour to her the black takes over from her face. You notice the black first. That is high contrast. Whereas the other image she is harmonising with the colours she is wearing.

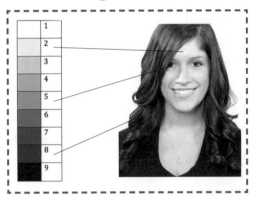

This girl has a higher level of contrast. While her skin is about the same shade, have you noticed how it appears lighter because her hair and eyes are so much darker?

Her hair is at level 8, her eyes are at level 5 and her skin is registering at level 2. In her case there is a total difference of 6 from her hair to her skin. There is also a difference of 3 between her eyes and skin. If she was to wear clothing close in colour to her skin there will be no harmony with her face. She really needs to wear a contrasting colour to liven up her image. See what happens when we put her into a light coloured top on the next page.

Now she has lost her intensity and looks pale in comparison. This girl does require a medium to high level of contrast.

To understand which level of contrast is best for you. Look at a photo of yourself next to the colour grids. There is a full page one at the back of the book to cut out or you can download one at the website www.latteslaughterandlipstick.com.au

Low levels of contrast occur when the maximum difference between your hair skin and eyes is under 2.

Medium levels of contrast occur when the maximum difference between your hair skin and eyes fall between 3 and 5.

High levels of contrast are required when the greatest difference between your hair skin or eyes is at 6 or more.

You may find that your hair and eyes are the same level but you look at the difference they make with your skin to gather your contrast levels.

The BLINK test

The safest way to check and see if what you are wearing is perfect for you or is taking over is to do the blink test.

I want you to finish reading these instructions before you try this test or your mind will create a picture that may not be accurate.

- Get up and stand in front of a mirror.
- Rather than look at your image close your eyes and clear your mind.
- Blink at yourself and see what remains or should I say imprints itself on your memory clearest.

Is it:

- Your face
- Your clothing
- Your jewellery

Or the fact that you are getting older and hate looking at yourself – well get over yourself. You are never again going to be as young as you are today so celebrate how gorgeous you are.

If the first thing that you noticed was your face then fabulous, you are wearing the right thing. If you noticed the colour or cut of your clothing then the clothing is wearing you and not the other way around.

Lastly if it is your jewellery that is fine if you want to have a signature piece stand out but again make sure that you are wearing the jewellery and it is not overtaking who you are.

Cool or warm?

The girls discovered that they were either cool or warm. Remember Louise looked no good in pastel pinks because she had a warm undertone to her colouring and Rebecca had definitely cool colouring so she looked great in the cool pinks, red and navies.

The simplest way to understand if your colouring is cooler or warmer is to either drape yourself in some gold or silver material. Now that can be hard to come by and the last thing you want to be doing is trying on gold or silver lurex to check out your colouring. In the absence of these colours you'll find you tend to wear more forest greens and warm or burnt oranges if you are warm and if you are cool you'll look amazing in pastel pinks and the nautical combinations of red, white and blue. There is a reason I have not mentioned black and brown here even though they are another two standards for defining warm and cool. That is because the number of women who insist on wearing black, especially in Melbourne, is out of control and I don't want you using black as a barometer for the temperature of your personal colouring. There are also numerous cool browns on the market so that too is of no help. Now if you find you primarily only wear black, this is also very common. Let me share this secret with you. If you have to do so with lashings of eye make-up to complete the look chances are you are too pale for black and it is not ideal. I hate to be the bearer of bad news but that black in your wardrobe may be making you older than your years as it does have that power as well. So by all means wear black if your hair or your skin or your eyes are dark, otherwise develop a love for charcoal or navy as both will be kinder to your complexion.

Action items for colour:

Look to discover which level of contrast you are. Then make sure you have clothing that reaches that level of contrast every day. It may be just the right shade of top of adding a jacket or piece of jewellery.

Do the blink test to make sure that you are wearing the right colours for you rather than them wearing you.

Get a feel for whether you are warm or cool and balance your wardrobe around that colour scheme.

Chapter B7.

Work your own wardrobe

Work your own wardrobe

Knowing what suits you and knowing what clothing to look for is great but the final piece of the puzzle is understanding how to store and find everything. Managing your wardrobe is imperative to making the most of everything that you have.

You may recall Cynthia had a wardrobe full or orphans, or outfits. Everything was spectacular on its own but had no relevance to anything else in the wardrobe. That is perfect if you can afford to live that way. The reality is most of us want clothing that will mix and match with many other items in our wardrobe. This chapter will show you how you can organise your wardrobe successfully. What to look for when you are shopping and what will be valuable in your wardrobe. Like eating, it is best to go shopping when you are not desperate for something new. You know it is impossible to shop when you are hungry you will come home with a trolley of items that will make you feel full in the short term but are not always the most nourishing for you. Shop when you have time, not a deadline, and you will be able to discern what you really can use as opposed to what is a quick fix for the day. That quick fix is destined for the goodwill bin within a very short period of time after you have done your penance and looked at it hanging unworn in your wardrobe for 6 to 12, maybe even 24 months.

Understand what your life looks like. Back in the first chapter of this How To sector you filled out a life chart to see where and how you spend your time. I want you to now return to that and highlight what you have written there in one colour for work, another colour for social, another colour for specific sports and a final colour for being at home, i.e. cooking, cleaning, watching telly.

By the amount of colour used for each section you can see if you spend more time out being social, at work in work clothes, being at home or playing specific sports. For example: If you work a forty hour week there will be travel time included which may bring your week in your work clothes up near 50 hours if you travel for 30 minutes or more a day. As we spend ideally eight hours sleep a night, you will then have

118 waking hours during the week. If you work or are in work clothes working and travelling that will account for close to 50% of your week. This means you should have 50% of your clothing wardrobe allocated to work clothes. It allows you freedom to be comfortable, happy and express your true self at work. Now if you wear a uniform then you do not have to worry about this percentage of your wardrobe. It is not factored in at all. All of your clothing will be for home and social occasions. The value in understanding how and where you spend your time helps you understand where you should spend your clothing budget. If you only work a few hours a week then you do not need to have a wardrobe full of suits.

Planning your wardrobe means you can have a very extensive wardrobe from only a few items. You can turn 12 garments into 96 outfits or potentially 120 if you like to show your upper arms.

Step one – Purchase two jackets.

Step two – Four bottoms to go with those two jackets. Every skirt, Capri or trouser you purchase must work with BOTH jackets.

Step three – Find three long sleeved tops that can be worn with camisoles and the three tops/shirts must suit all of the pieces in step one and step two.

Step four – Look for three camisoles that can be worn under every shirt to give it a different look.

The combinations of all of those above items can create 120 different outfits.

If you find this confusing then ensure that any time you buy anything that it WILL co-ordinate with at least two other pieces that you already have at home. Nothing is of value if by purchasing it you have to buy the pants, shoes and handbag or top to match.

Also never purchase anything where the salesperson tells you with the right lipstick it will look great. Basically they have told you that it doesn't really suit you but you can make it work. You want to roll out of bed on your worst morning and know that you look great even before you have applied any make-up.

Now that you know your lifestyle and your personality it is time to sort through your wardrobe. Toss everything that you have onto your bed into three piles.

- Pile #1 – it fits, I love it, it's perfect.
- Pile #2 – there is something not quite right, the colour, the fit, it is an orphan
- Pile #3 – it doesn't fit, it looks dreadful OR I never wear it.

Pile #1 goes back into the cupboard; Pile #3 goes straight out the door. It is a complete waste of your valuable wardrobe space. If it happens to be your prom dress or something special you can hang it in another wardrobe or even place it in safe keeping in a storage container or a vacuum sealed bag. Pile #2 – You have to decide if the garment can be saved by alterations, or mixing it with the right colours or purchasing something to go with it.

You must now start creating a list of what you need immediately, in six months or if the right piece is at exactly the right price but it isn't urgent.

When you know what is missing that is a great time to go shopping especially at the sales. You have a purpose, some may even say a mission and you know what you are after. Buying on a whim can be expensive especially if the said item is half or a quarter of its asking price and you still have no use for it.

A good rule of thumb is anything that is classical in nature, good jackets, pants or shoes you can afford spending a bit more on as you will have the item for a while. Something that is a trend but you know will be here and gone in a couple of years you will spend a bit less on and you only spend a token amount on anything that is a passing fad. Gladiator sandals are such a fad. They will last two seasons and then be related to a particular year and be out of fashion, quickly replaced by something new. Don't overspend on these items. Grab a couple of lower priced pieces to give you a fashionable look but don't blow your budget.

Setting up your wardrobe

I hear many people sort their wardrobe with reference to colour, my girlfriend Ronel Fourie, another Image Consultant, showed me this other more sensible layout.

Store and hang your clothing into its occasion. Keep all of your work clothes together; keep your social clothes together and your special event clothing in their own separate section. Potentially even in another room if you have the space. This way you can go straight to the event rather than sorting through the colour. I find having my clothes arranged according to the event, allows me to see where my gaps are much easier than if it was sorted according to colour. In my case this works as my life is filled with different events. Should your life be less about requiring different clothing for events then I would suggest you sort it according to colour or garment. My work and presentation outfits are at the end of my wardrobe and my everyday clothes are up near the front as I can wear everyday clothing when I am working from home and I keep my suits and more formal clothes separated for those occasions only.

Travelling wardrobes

The girls gave Louise a hand to organise her weekend away. When you are travelling plan what you are going to pack. Do not just pack at the last minute. It means like shopping you will throw a load of unwanted weight into your case and take up the valuable space that your new treasures will need on your return journey.

Earlier this chapter I explained how 12 pieces can create 120 outfits. This is the formula you want to work with to fill any overnight or weekend away bag. Only for a weekend you will not require as many pieces.

I once attended a conference with a piece of luggage that was no larger than a cosmetics case. I arrived Friday in trousers, with a top and long knit jacket. That evening I put on a new top. The second day I had spare trousers and top in my case. I wore the long knit jacket again. That evening I wore a jersey knit full length evening dress with fresh evening heels. The last day I wore the same trousers I had worn the first day, a fresh top and the wrap I had worn with my dress the evening before. In all, my bag contained two pairs of shoes, a pair of trousers, three tops, an evening dress, a wrap, make-up, underwear and jewellery. It is very easy to pack light if you plan well.

By using dry cleaning bags you can minimise creases in your clothing and if you have to pack your trousers into a case pack them into the bottom of your case first with the end of the legs hanging out of the case. Build up your layers of clothing and finish packing your trousers over your clothing. It helps to eliminate a sharp crease half way down your legs.

The final word on wardrobes.

Use good quality hangers and tools to store your clothing and accessories. Get rid of the nasty wire hangers, they do not hold shape in your garments nor do they allow your clothing to breathe properly. When you can get air moving around your clothing they stay fresher longer and will last longer.

Action items for building up a great wardrobe of clothing.

Shop when you have time on your side.

Buy what is relevant to your needs. Create a plan and stick to it.

Whatever you buy must go with two existing items in your wardrobe.

Personal colour contrast grid

1	
2	
3	
4	
5	
6	
7	
8	
9	